I WANNA BE A SALES REP

I WANNA BE A SALES REP

The Insider's Guide to Landing

Great-Paying Jobs in Sales

Lydia Afeman

SCS

Book design by Mark McGarry
Set in Goudy

Library of Congress Catalog Card Number

9 8 7 6 5 4 3 2 1
Printed in the United States of America

Lydia Afeman
P.O. Box 1141
Addison, TX 75001-1141
(972)-38-SALES fax, phone
afemanl@aol.com

DISCLAIMER OF LIABILITY AND WARRANTY
This publication describes the author's opinion regarding the subject matter herein. It is sold with the understanding that the publisher and author are not engaged in rendering any professional service. If expert assistance is required, the services of a qualified professional should be obtained.

The author and publisher assume no responsibility whatsoever for the uses made of this material or for decisions based on its use, and make no warranties, either express or implied, regarding the contents of this book. The author and publisher specifically disclaim any liability, loss or risk incurred directly, indirectly or incidentally as a consequence of the use and/or application of any advice or information

In loving memory of my father,
who was a born sales rep.

Contents

Acknowledgments   ix
Introduction   xi

1

I Wanted to be a Sales Rep:
A Job Success Story

1

2

Networking with Reps and Managers:
Where to Track Them Down

17

3

Talking to Contacts:
Getting Useful Information

35

4

Getting Your Foot in the Door:
Creating Opportunities for Experience

49

5

Developing Sales Skills:
Professional Sales Training Courses
67

6

Selling Yourself:
Tips for Attention-Grabbing Resumes
81

7

Securing an Interview:
It's Not What You Know...
99

8

Knowing How to Answer:
Finding Out What Interviewing Managers Expect
109

9

Knowing What to Ask:
Researching a Company Before an Interview
133

10

Winning the Job:
Preparing a Marketing Strategy to Present
at the Interview
151

11

Final Advice:
Avoiding Pitfalls and Outwitting Shark
159

Acknowledgments

I<small>T IS APPROPRIATE THAT MY FIRST MESSAGE IS A PERSONAL</small> one, acknowledging the efforts of a special group of individuals whose expertise, encouragement, and response to endless requests for information made this book possible.

Many of the stories in this book were generously told by busy sales reps out in the field who kindly stopped to answer my question: How did you land your first position in sales? To the many that answered my questions, thank you for the stories, strategies, and information that I am passing on to those who are starting out as we did. Thanks, too, to my sales managers for hiring me and giving me the fourteen years of experience that made this book possible.

This book was a labor of love, and the loved ones who supported me are my mother, my aunt, and my friends. One friend in particular helped me get started: Floyd Bonner urged me to write the book myself after months of my trying to convince him to ghostwrite it for me. Another very special person—an angel—is Bernie

Watring, who provided information on a second's notice for many of the chapters in this book. Without her I would be months away from finishing this book.

Thanks also go to Becky Thompson, who performed the needed research and polished my quickly written chapters to hand to my editor, Jason Rath. Jason's gifted talents for editing were brought to this project by prayer. If all my prayers could be answered like this one, I would be the luckiest person on earth.

Special thanks go to Mark McGarry, whose design made this book a reality, to John Baird, whose cover design made me proud to say I wrote this book, and to Kathryn McKay, who took it to the finish line. Thanks also to Gail Nogle for her excellant photography.

Finally, to H.K., I believe we meet certain people along life's path for a reason. Without having met you, I may never have written this book and fulfilled my life's dream.

Introduction

SALES, A HIGHLY COMPETITIVE FIELD WITH LUCRATIVE benefits like travel, high salaries, commissions, and bonuses, is attracting ever-increasing numbers of driven, professionally minded people. A Bureau of Labor Statistics report estimates that there are currently close to 3 million sales jobs in the United States. That number is expected to experience above-average growth through the year 2005, representing a remarkable thirty-eight percent growth within the next ten years. J. Michael Farr, author of the *The 50 Fastest Growing Jobs*, estimates an average numerical growth of more than 430,000 new sales positions *every year*.

I wrote *I Wanna Be A Sales Rep!* with this information in mind, hoping to benefit four key groups:

- College students and graduates looking for entry-level sales positions;
- Current sales reps wanting to change jobs or fields;
- Career changers (nurses, lawyers, engineers, pharmacists, teachers, university professors, architects, accountants,

medical technologists, lab techs, social workers, women re-entering the job market, self-employers, etc.);
* Job recruiters, outplacement firms, career counselors, and college placement offices.

There are more than 14.4 million students enrolled in over 3,600 college and universities across the country, and interest in business careers is on the rise. By the year 2000, bachelor's degrees will be conferred to an all-time-high 1.2 million job-seekers, a huge proportion of which will be in business-related fields. In addition, these students will graduate into a job market where over a quarter of twenty-four- to forty-four-year-olds has four or more years of college education. With such stiff competition for jobs after graduation, students need in-depth job-search tips and the competitive edge that *I Wanna Be A Sales Rep* has to offer.

The Census Bureau estimates that approximately ten percent of employees change jobs every year. Several surveys suggest that about sixty percent of these moves occur within the same occupational category. That means that if there are currently 3 million sales reps in the United States, approximately 180,000 of them will look for new sales jobs every year. With numbers of career changers and graduates entering the sales field steadily on the rise—and with their job-search techniques becoming increasingly sophisticated—current reps planning a job change within the field must look for ways to hone their job-search and interviewing skills to compete.

As for other job-changers, twenty percent will move to entirely different fields, a number representing hundreds of thousand of job-seekers. Surveys show that the primary motivations behind these career shifts are earning potential and growth rewards. With sales ranking high in both areas, the field is a hot target for a huge segment of this particular market. Considering the majority of career changers have higher levels of education than those who don't move, this large segment of individuals must be equipped with enough information and tools to compete in the job arena.

In addition, growing numbers of women are entering or re-entering the workforce at midlife or are changing careers. These women are attracted to the sales field and seeking out many of the available positions. In fact, the number of women in sales positions has increased from six percent in 1986 to an all time high of thirty-five percent in 1996 and is expected to steadily increase into the year 2000. It's my hope that *I Wanna Be A Sales Rep!* will give these women the edge they need to succeed in such a competitive arena.

Recruiters are inundated by callers inquiring about sales positions and how to land them. These staffing professionals need reference sources they can recommend so that these requests do not take up valuable recruiting time. Career counselors, too, whether working in private practice or in university career placement offices, can benefit from the solid, up-to-date information found in this book.

No matter which group you fall into, however, you are most likely looking for a comprehensive volume containing all the information required to launch a career in sales—from resume writing to salary negotiation. If you have experienced the frustration of attempting to find that first sales job, agonized over performing poorly on an interview, finding a position can be far more difficult than you imagined. The beauty of the strategies presented in this book is that they are straightforward and practical. You'll find do-able ideas that don't call for the kind of unrealistic self-sacrifice that causes many people to give up their search.

Although there are many other books that focus on resumes, cover letters, interviewing, and general job-search strategies, this is the first to be tailored to the needs of readers searching for jobs in sales. You'd have to buy ten of these other books and sift though hundreds of pages of irrelevant information to get even half the facts and advice contained in *I Wanna Be A Sales Rep.*

There are several reasons I wrote this book. Mainly it was because I had such a difficult time finding my first position more than a decade ago. I wrote the book that I wish someone had given to me during my junior year in college. But I was also motivated to answer the people I met who kept asking the same question, "How did you break into sales?" These were mostly strangers who wanted to know the secrets to finding a position in sales. After seven years in sales, I received a call from an attorney in the midst of a career change looking for advice on how to make the transition from law to sales. After spending an hour giving her pointers on how to get started, she told me that she had consulted professionals—professionals she paid—and I was the only person who gave her any real solid information she could use. She asked me "Why don't you write a book about how to break into sales?" I was so surprised that my advice was better than what she had actually paid experts for. At that point I decided to write this book, a book that job-seekers could really use. It took seven more years to collect all of the information contained in these pages.

> Sometimes we think we are committed and we aren't. A chicken and a pig were talking about commitment. The chicken said, "I'm committed to giving eggs every morning." The pig said, "Giving eggs isn't commitment, it's participation. Giving ham is total commitment!"
>
> *Anonymous*

This book includes a wide variety of stories about searching for that first job that I had collected from experienced reps I'd met in the field. Most of these were scribbled on napkins, pieces of paper, the backs of business cards, and sheets torn out of my dayplanner. These successful candidates' strategies are offered throughout the book. You'll read in Chapter One how a total stranger offered me the guidance I needed to find my first position. I wrote this book to offer newcomers the same kind of essential "insider information" I received from my mentor. The result is this step-by-step manual packed with field-specific tips and information to guide you through the intricacies of landing that first sales job. This book is based in practice, not theory—the information presented comes from success on the job-search battlefield, from the know-how that is the result of years of experience, and from years of interviewing others in the trenches.

Each of the following chapters is packed with ideas and strategies to help you:

1. Make contact with people in the industry,
2. Create opportunities to gain the experience you need,
3. Win interviews, and ultimately,
4. Land a sales position.

But remember that there is a lot of work to be done. If you are truly sales rep material, you will digest this information, then draw on it to land that first position. Good luck!

The salesperson sells cars, tractors, radios, televisions, iceboxes and movies, health and leisure, ambition and fulfillment.

The salesperson is America's emissary of abundance, Mr. and Mrs. High-Standard-of-Living in person.

They ring the billion doorbells and enrich a billion lives. Without them there'd be no American ships at sea, no busy factories, no sixty million jobs.

For the great American salesperson is the great American civilizer, and everywhere they go they leave people better off.

John Hancock Mutual Life

I Wanted to be a Sales Rep:
A Job Search Success Story

HAVING BEEN IN THE SAME STRAITS—TRYING TO find that first entry-level sales position—more than a decade ago, I can empathize with those hunting down their first sales job. I remember the pain of being rejected during an interview and the bewilderment of not knowing how to overcome the objections raised by the interviewer. Not until one day, flying back from yet another failed interview, was I lucky enough to meet on the airplane a sales manager working in the medical field. This generous man gave me practical answers to the difficult problems inherent in the search for that first sales position. The story he related became the key to my success in landing my first sales position.

The issues that other reps and I faced then are the same issues that career changers and graduating students face today. The only difference is that there is more competition now for these positions than ever before. As companies downsize, sales representatives are being laid off. In fact, many large companies have dropped their entire direct sales force, and have instead contracted with distributors, who sell lines from a variety of companies, to represent their lines.

Today, you need every tool you can acquire to find a sales position. This book is designed to equip the entry-level candidate with practical information and multiple strategies so that he can compete on the same turf as experienced candidates.

Why do so many people want to get into sales? First, selling can be very lucrative: Even entry-level sales positions can offer substantial monetary rewards. Most companies offer a base salary, commission or bonus, use of a company car or car allowance, and benefits. Benefits often include medical, dental, disability, life insurance, child care, education reimbursement, retirement, 401k, credit union, and intercompany loans. Even stock options are sometimes offered. The perks vary depending on the field entered and how well one negotiates. Second, selling is a way to fulfill the desire to be affiliated with a prestigious national company. After all, sales representatives are critical to a company's success: They introduce new or existing product lines to the marketplace, convert clients to their company's products or services, sustain and increase market share, penetrate difficult markets, and encourage product loyalty. Finally, many people like to set their own schedules and to work at their own pace.

"The power of your ambition depends wholly on the vigor of the determination behind it. What you accomplish will depend on the amount of live energy, of enthusiasm, and willpower you put into your efforts to achieve."

Randy D. Marsh

Have you wondered what it would be like to pursue a career in sales? Have you contemplated looking for a sales position? Do you know where to begin? Have you been told it is hard to break into the industry without some sales experience? Have you been unsuccessful at either getting that first interview or being called back for a follow-up interview? Have you been turned down time after time because you lack the necessary sales experience?

Here's a step-by-step approach on how to overcome the fierce competition for these entry-level positions. These techniques are applicable to almost any sales field. I've received enthusiastic responses from the candidates I've taught in the past, and I feel that sharing this information may help future sales candidates prepare better for the challenge of finding a job in the '90s and beyond.

MY STORY

When I was looking for my first sales representative position, I didn't anticipate the obstacles that faced me. The search turned out to be a dispiriting experience. I had looked forward to graduating with a B.A. in marketing in May 1983. With dreams of the future in full bloom and a goal set in the medical sales field, I composed my resume in October 1982. The only advice I had received about finding an entry-level sales position was to start sending out resumes six to nine months prior to graduation. I did what I thought was the key to landing a job before graduation: I sent out more than three hundred resumes—one to each and every medical and pharmaceutical company listed in the Loyola University card catalog file and in the Physicians Desk Reference or PDR, as it is called. It was the month of November, and I thought I was right on track.

Disappointingly, in December, the rejection letters started pouring in. Merry Christmas! Every letter said the same thing: "Thank you for your interest in our company. Although your qualifications are admirable, you lack the necessary sales experience required for this position." I kept thinking, "No one told me I needed experience!" The crux of my problem in finding a position was lack of experience in medical or any other type of sales.

Undaunted, I barked up other trees. I answered every sales ad in the classified section of the newspaper, not just medical company want ads. I also phoned every recruiter in New Orleans, begging for an interview for a sales position. By May, I'd gone on so many second-rate interviews that the natty little business suit I'd bought for these question and answer sessions was becoming threadbare. I was never asked back for a second interview, and the rejection letters kept coming. The only real reason for my repeated rejections was my lack of sales experience.

> "Be like a postage stamp. Stick to something until you get there."
>
> *Josh Billings*

By the end of June 1983, I was still unemployed and feeling as if I were never going to find a position. But I am tenacious: Being told "No" only made me more determined to get the one "Yes" that I needed to set my sales career in motion.

One day, I received a call from one of the recruiters I'd been calling for months to help me locate an entry-level position. The recruiter had scheduled an interview for me with a company based in Dallas that was hiring a rep to sell advertising to companies in the oil industry. The position was based in New Orleans, and the job required calling on oil-related businesses in Louisiana. I convinced this inexperienced recruiter to help me, but he was as much a novice at recruiting as I was at sales: He failed to mention that the manager did not have a copy of my resume, and he advised me to just sell the manager on the fact that I wanted this position and was willing to learn the ropes of the industry. The next day I flew to Dallas for the interview. (The company paid for my flight and expenses.) After the manager read my resume, we talked for a mere twenty minutes before I was ushered out and given cab fare back to the airport. In the cab, I was so humiliated I felt like screaming. When I arrived at the airport, I went directly to my gate and caught an earlier flight back to New Orleans. I boarded the plane, sat in my seat and began to cry. I did not care who saw me because by now my suit was wrinkled, and I had to keep my feet flat on the floor to hide the holes in the soles of my shoes. I was so tired of rejection, I wanted to give up, then and there.

My Anonymous Mentor

The next thing I was aware of was a gentleman leaning across the aisle to ask why I was crying. When I looked up, I saw a truly concerned face. I choked out the story about the interview and the "Catch 22" of selling—that I could not find a sales position because I lacked the necessary sales experience, but to gain experience you needed to have a sales position. He told me he understood. In fact, he said, he was a sales manager for a medical company.

"Really?" I asked in amazement. When he asked me whether I would like to hear some advice about securing an entry-level sales position, I was almost overcome with appreciation.

His story provided a true life example of what to anticipate, how to handle different situations, and how to package myself for a potential employer. I was captivated by the advice he gave. This kind gentleman's story served as both an inspiration and a springboard for me to redirect and refocus the efforts of my job search. In that hour and a half flight, I learned what I'd been doing wrong for almost eight months.

This is the story he told me: At the end

> "Mentors...guide their disciples...imparting the wisdom they have acquired over many years...godfathers (sometimes called "rabbis") are in a position to intervene on your behalf; by definition, they are powerful people with an interest in your career."
>
> Managing Up, Managing Down *by Mary Ann Allison, vice president, CitiCorp; and Eric Allison, financial writer.*

5

of his sophomore year of college, he decided he wanted to be a medical sales representative. At the end of the semester, he began spending free time in the library researching medical companies. He also went to the local hospital, waited in the lobby, and watched as the reps came in from the parking lot to use the phone before making their sales calls. He would approach those who were between calls and strike up a conversation with them, asking as many questions as possible to obtain the information he needed to start his career search. By coming prepared with a list of questions, he was able to efficiently take down the information he needed for the day he would be interviewed. He emphasized the importance of obtaining information from people with sales experience. Some examples of his questions were:

- What do you do on an average day as a sales rep?
- How did you get into sales?
- What did you say to the interviewer that clinched your first sales position?

When the sales reps asked him why he was asking these questions, he told them he needed firsthand information from experienced sales reps for a term paper he was writing entitled "Job Hunting in the Sales Field."

I was amazed that he had the courage to stop people in the lobby of a hospital and pose these questions. But it gets even better. Upon completion of his "research," he called five companies for whom he wanted to work. A couple of the companies he contacted he had heard about from the sales reps at the hospital. He told each of the companies that he was a college student doing research for a term paper. As he contacted the companies he asked all kinds of questions. He found out the names of the people reps called on while at the hospitals, the type of sales reps they hired, which products the companies sold, and more. After he elicited as much information as he could from the companies, he telephoned the hospitals. Even though he had no clue what to do or say, he used the term paper story throughout the entire process. He learned that people are prone to be sympathetic with a student who is "conducting research." He started a workbook and filed the information he collected.

My mentor scheduled appointments with several nurses and doctors who used products from the companies with whom he had spoken. Next, he made up lists of questions he wanted answered about the company, its products, and its sales reps, as well as about the reasons these doctors and nurses bought and used the particular products they did.

During each call, he took copious notes. He asked the doctor or nurse as many questions as time allowed. He made a point of sending a thank-you letter to each person he had interviewed at the hospital. By now, his notebook was starting to overflow with information about the needs and preferences of the customers—the things they liked the sales reps to do for them while at the hospital.

After he finished interviewing a doctor or nurse, he would ask him for his sales rep's name and phone number. Then he contacted the sales rep. He explained to the rep that he had received her name from one of her customers. This always got the rep's attention. He would tell her why he was calling and why he had interviewed personnel at the hospital—the term paper story. He would ask the rep to meet with him at one of the hospitals she called on, so that he could observe an average day in the field. He always showed up for his appointments dressed as a professional in a business suit to make the rep feel comfortable with his appearance. It was the only suit he had—a nice one he had bought on sale—and he made good use of it. He told me that reps selling medical products observe surgical procedures in order to instruct doctors on the use of the products. They take advantage of this time with the doctor to sell him other products. After becoming better

7

acquainted with some of the reps, he was able to get clearance with the doctors to observe one or more procedures.

When he could arrange to meet a rep at the hospital, they would often run into other reps in the halls, at the pay phones, and in the elevators. Sometimes some of these reps were with their managers. Seizing every opportunity, he started collecting business cards from each rep he met. Given the opportunity, he asked each rep how he landed his first sales position—information he needed for a that term paper. He laughed. That term paper story sure got him a lot of mileage.

If he and a rep hit it off, the rep might take him to lunch. Generally, they ate at one of the delis near the hospital where other medical and pharmaceutical reps often ate. He had a field day asking questions of every rep he met. One thing about reps, he said, is they love to talk about their success. "And so do sales managers," I thought to myself. Following lunch, they would make several sales calls and finish work in the afternoon. At the end of the day, he would obtain the name and address of the rep's manager. He faithfully followed up with thank-you letters and often volunteered his time to return the favor to the reps.

Armed now with information, research material, interview experience with doctors and nurses, phone-interview experience with company personnel, in-depth interviews with sales reps, and observation of medical procedures, he began a two-year campaign to gain employment with one of five targeted companies. He commented that he had learned enough about each company to sound knowledgeable in an interview. "I trained myself and obtained the necessary experience on my own," he said. That was the solution to the problem: If you can't find an internship to help you gain experience, then create your own.

For the next two years, he read sales books, took sales courses, and worked in a part-time sales position. He learned as much about sales and the medical industry as he could. In addition, he kept up a steady mail campaign directed to his contact list of reps and managers. On occasion, he helped the reps out. He sent Christmas cards, letters, and copies of his grades. He wrote letters to the managers expressing his desire after graduation to interview for a sales position. He mentioned to them that he had done research and observed reps at work on a day-to-day basis. Upon graduation, he sent each rep and manager a graduation announcement, a resume, and a cover letter.

Fortunately, a rep who was being promoted recommended him as his replacement. A month later, another rep left for a position at another company and also recommended him as his replacement. He landed both interviews and received both offers. I was amazed but not surprised that he was now a sales manager. "You have to play the game," he told me. "You need to know the market, develop background information, cultivate connections, and determine what the customer wants and needs. Being creative and being at the right place at the right time is half the battle."

As we disembarked from the plane, he told me, "It is a lot harder nowadays to find a position, but remember my story and create your own opportunity. As a sales manager, I often hire my medical reps from the consumer sales industry. Consumer sales is a good training ground for entry-level medical reps—perhaps you can get your start there." His parting comment to me was, "If you are truly rep material, you will use this information I have given you, and you will find a position."

I thanked him for telling me his wonderful story. I felt indebted to this stranger for sharing his story, because until then, no one else had helped me. As he glanced at his watch, then hurried off to make his connecting flight, I realized I didn't even know his name. Nonetheless, the story told by this anonymous mentor provided the knowledge and inspiration I needed to develop my own game plan to find that first sales position.

MAKING CONTACT

When I arrived in New Orleans after my failed interview, for the first time in months, the drive home was not depressing. After my conversation with the man on the plane, I finally felt I had the necessary information and guidance to enable me to find a real sales position.

On my way home, I stopped at the grocery store. There, standing in the toothpaste aisle, was a sales rep who worked for an over-the-counter drug company. I walked right up to her and boldly asked, "Are you a sales rep?" She smiled and said, "Yes, I am." This was my lucky day, I thought. It occurred to me that it was going to be easier than I expected to seek out sales reps. I told her that I had just graduated from college and was looking for a sales position. She told me she knew exactly what I was going through, because she had been with her company for only a year—she was fresh out of college.

> "A single conversation across the table with a wise man is better than ten years' study of books."
>
> Henry Wadsworth Longfellow

As we talked, I asked her advice about where to go to find consumer goods company reps and how to go about making contacts. I asked her to describe her job responsibilities and what she did on a typical day. Finally, I asked if she knew any company that had open positions for entry-level candidates like me. She gave me her business card and asked me to call her after she had some time to think about my questions. I told her I would and I took her card, intending to call in a few days. I hardly realized it at the time, but I had just made my first contact.

Once home, I decided to develop a strategy and to set goals based upon my resources and time. Needless to say, I had more time than resources at this juncture. I was house-sitting for a friend for a month, and I was working at another friend's boutique, but I was making barely enough money to eat. Another resume mailer was financially out of the question.

That night, however, I realized I had more resources than I had thought. My friend's kitchen, it occurred to me, was a veritable library of consumer companies. Products from virtually every major packaged goods company were lined up on the shelves of her pantry. I started making a list of every item, brand, and company name represented on the shelves. By the end of the night, I had an impressive list. The next day I started calling grocery and drug stores to garner additional information.

When I later telephoned the sales rep whom I had met at the supermarket, she gave me an excellent lead on where to find several sales reps and sales managers gathered at one time. She directed me to one of the busiest drug stores in the city. On Thursdays, she said, reps went to the store to present their products and promotions to the buyers. The next day, I phoned the manager of the store and asked him several questions:

- What do the reps do while they are in the store?
- Describe to me what the perfect rep does to win your business?
- If I were a rep, how would I get an appointment with you?
- What would you want a sales rep not to do?

He told me the store closes on Thursday afternoons, allowing time for the reps to present to him new products and promotions and to ask for permission to build displays. This time is also used to rotate the stock, pick up damaged and out-of-date merchandise, and to compete for more shelf space and facings.

THE UMBRELLA TRICK

The following Thursday, I arrived with resume in hand, just as the reps began pouring into the store. They were sopping wet because it was pouring down rain. Digging in their trunks and dragging in their briefcases, displays, and products, they ran in the store soaked to the bone, not in the mood to talk to me about anything.

After about thirty minutes, I decided to go to the local department store, pick up two umbrellas and return to the scene of soaking wet reps. As they had arrived, I realized not one of them seemed to possess an umbrella.

"The way I see it, if you want the rainbow you have to put up with the rain."

Dolly Parton

Each time a rep drove up, I would wait until he started digging in his trunk. Then I would walk over to him carrying the two umbrellas. I would hold one over the rep's head while he bent over his trunk to unload his paraphernalia. I politely asked if he could use a hand or an umbrella. No one ever turned me down. I walked with each sales rep into the store, holding high the two opened umbrellas.

During this procedure, each rep asked the same question, "What are you doing standing in the parking lot with two umbrellas?" I explained to the reps that I was looking for a sales position and wanted to learn firsthand what work they do as reps in the field. I wanted to be a sales rep, and since I did not know how, I was training myself. I told them that I had been looking for a position since the previous October and that I had graduated from college in May. They were so surprised by my response that each one said he would try to help me.

CREATING EXPERIENCE

Now that I had begun making a number of contacts in the field I set about creating the experience I needed on my resume to land a job. I asked the reps I had met if I could help them rotate stock and build their displays. I asked each one if I could come back and help them again some time. Some of them let me listen to the sales presentations they made to the buyers. I collected business cards so that I could call the reps later to see if they had any leads on sales positions.

One especially nice fellow took me around the store and explained to me what the reps were doing and why. It turned out he was not a rep, but a sales manager. Bingo! I asked him, "Why do you hire one rep over another? What is it you look for in a rep?" He answered, "People like you who stand in the rain with umbrellas looking for a position." As it turned out, he did not have any openings, but he took a copy of my resume, and I added his card to my growing file.

> "A winner is someone who recognizes his God-given talents, works his tail off to develop them into skills, and uses these skills to accomplish his goals."
>
> *Larry Bird, professional basketball player*

I began to receive calls and phone screens from sales managers for sales territories. I kept up my weekly visits to the drug store to make contacts. I also went to the headquarters of a couple of supermarket chains to do the same thing. I was not giving up. Soon, I had learned exactly what a consumer sales rep's position involved and the details of his day.

Every time I went to a store, I kept my eyes open for sales reps. I could spot one ten miles away. My notebook began to fill up with information. I had notes, business cards, and clippings of the newspaper advertisements I had responded to. As I looked for a position, I continued to pursue traditional avenues—calling recruiters, sending in resumes in response to advertisements in the newspaper, and telephoning sales reps I had met to find out leads on positions.

One evening, I had a message on my answering machine from Doug Norton, the Divisional Manager of Martha White Foods, a division of Beatrice Foods. He had run an ad in the newspaper that I had responded to a few months earlier. He had kept my resume and the cover letter I had sent in response to the ad. Talk about timing! There was an opening for a sales position in Baton Rouge. He asked me whether I would come to his office for an interview. How do you think I responded? Yes! Yes! Yes!

I met Doug the next morning at eight o'clock sharp. I was so excited I could hardly sit in the chair. He asked me each of the questions I had been asking all the reps for the past few months. Finally, after a whole year, I was armed with the answers that he wanted to hear. All those days of hanging out in parking lots, interviewing and observing reps were finally paying off. I had trained myself and created my own internship. As my mentor had, I too had read so many sales books, I sounded as though I had more experience than I actually did.

"Become the most positive and enthusiastic person you know."

Life's Little Instruction Book

The next day, Doug made me an offer. My starting salary was sixteen thousand dollars a year, the use of a company car, and benefits, which at the time was not a bad entry-level package. A perk of four dollars per day for lunch was included. Wow! This was October 1983, exactly one year after I sent out my first resume. It had taken a year—and a long year at that. Looking back, I realized that if I had been better prepared for that first position, I could have shortened my search. But I was learning with each experience, no matter how pleasant or painful.

I sold Martha White products—flour meal and grits—to grocery stores. The first week on the job, I went with Doug into stores to clean out shelves, rotate stock, and place marketing tags on the products. I worked very hard to be successful. During this time, I received several complimentary letters that I placed in a file at home that I called my "Atta-Way File." I kept all the letters in which I'd received praise in this file. For instance, when Doug would jot me a note, "That was a great display at Schwegmanns's,"

I put it in my special file. I had my Atta-Way File spiral bound to take along on future interviews. I wanted my resume to reflect that I had the potential to land a position in medical sales some day. After a year of stocking shelves and selling flour displays, I was ready to move on and hopefully land that first medical sales position.

Where do you think I spent some of my spare time after I finished my day with Martha White? Right—in hospital parking lots on rainy days.

One day I read an ad in a newspaper for an entry-level position placed by a medical recruiter. During our meeting, I was surprised to learn that the recruiter felt my one sales position with Martha White was sufficient to convince the manager of The Kendall Company, a medical supplier, to grant me an interview. If I could sell flour meal and grits, the recruiter told the manager, I could certainly sell T.E.D. antiembolism stockings for reducing deep vein thrombosis. I was elated when the manager agreed to an interview, but I was told he was looking for two years of sales experience. I had one shot at the job, and I knew I had to make it count.

> "All experience is an arch, to build upon."
>
> *Henry Brooks Adams,*
> *American writer*
> *and historian*

The manager, Scott Stallets, was well over six feet tall. When I met him, I was so intimidated that my knees shook. He made it clear he was not planning to hire me as a charity case; he wanted results. He picked apart my single year of sales experience, but I came back at him with an answer every time. Also, I handed Scott my Atta-Way File. The letters of commendation and praise added weight to my resume and put me ahead of the other candidates. I believe that file gave me the edge I needed to overcome the limitation of just one year of experience. I went home exhausted from the interview, but I was his number one candidate.

The position was put on temporary hold. Over the next several months, Scott asked me in for another interview . . . and another. He was testing my determination because that was what the position called for. He had to be convinced I would not take no for an answer.

When I landed the position, I was on cloud nine. My first position in medical sales! The only sad part was having to inform Doug and his wife that I was leaving the Martha White Company. Doug had been a great influence on me that year. I worked hard for him because he was fair, honest, moral, and full of integrity. I was lucky to have had a manager of his caliber as my first experience with management.

> "We succeed only as we identify in life, or in war, or in anything else, a single overriding objective, and make all other considerations bend to that one objective."
>
> *Dwight D. Eisenhower*

Scott, too, turned out to be a pleasant person to work for. I was lucky—two excellent supervisors in a row. I was doing a great job. I was converting accounts left and right, yet I realized I still did not know much about sales. It was my good fortune that The Kendall Company put me through an extensive sales training course. After that, with my sales numbers and income rising rapidly, Scott nicknamed me the T.E.D. Hit Lady. I was finally on my way.

2

Networking with Reps and Managers: Where to Track Them Down

WHEN I SET OUT ON MY FIRST SEARCH FOR A SALES job, the hardest part was knowing where to begin. How could I get answers to my many questions about the sales field and how to land a job in it if I didn't even know whom to ask? The best people to ask, of course, are those who are already working in the field. But in the beginning, I had no idea where I could even *find* these people. Although standing in parking lots with umbrellas eventually worked for me, I realize with hindsight the many other methods I might have used to meet sales reps and managers.

Making contact with those directly affiliated with your sphere of interest is an ideal way of entering the sales field. The relationships you develop will become valuable job reference sources. Through them, you will find positions faster than will job-seekers without contacts, and you will

> "To get ahead . . . learn from others with proven success and experience. Don't be afraid to adopt key parts of their styles."
>
> *Sharron Lipscomb, Special Assistant, U.S. Department of Justice Management*

keep one step ahead of the pack. You will learn which jobs are becoming available, and you will have inside knowledge about which companies are hiring and which are not. Another advantage is that you can find out which companies offer internships, use part-time sales people, hire flex-time sales people, or are more likely to offer entry-level sales positions. Furthermore, you will gain insight from experienced sales people as to what is involved in selling to the particular industry you wish to enter. As you develop your relationship with your contacts, you may even have the opportunity to observe them at work in the field, enabling you to actually see what sales reps do every day.

Chances are, if you do not work especially hard at this stage of your job search, you will become discouraged and abandon your dream of attaining a sales position. It is easier to find sales reps than you may imagine. You'll need to keep your eyes open and look for opportunities to find sales reps on a daily basis. Keep a record of anyone you meet who is in sales—always ask for a business card and cross-reference by industry and company.

"Networking is being able to help or benefit from individuals you directly have a relationship with to achieve life's ends."

Paul Drolson, division manager, American Express

Whether you want to meet reps for consumer, computer, clothing, furniture, medical, or other industries, the process is the same. The main point is that wherever you are, take the opportunity to meet new people and make a point of figuring out where the reps are. You never know whom you will meet or when someone may lead you to an ideal job opportunity.

SEMINARS AND SALES TRAINING CLASSES

Chapter Five discusses the advantages of attending one-day seminars and sales training classes. Many sales professionals take classes to improve their skills and make friends with other professionals in their fields. If you enroll in a sales training class, you'll meet and interact with salespersons in a group setting. You may want to ask the training consultant to enroll you in a class that has a large number of sales representatives in the field you have targeted. Remember, you are paying for the course, so you want to use every dollar spent to gain experience and make contacts with those who can help you move one step closer to your goal.

Explain to the training consultant your goals. Ask how many reps are enrolled in the course, and in which fields they work. Make sure you are surrounded by the people you want to reach. Although you may have to wait to take a class that has a higher enrollment of sales professionals, there is no sense in settling for a course that will not help you make contacts while you undergo training. Another plus to training with reps experienced in your field of interest is that when the class discusses sales topics, the case studies and examples are more likely to have direct relevance to your own specific career goals.

> *What makes achievement possible in business?*
> "Being willing to learn new things, being able to assimilate new information quickly, and being able to get along with and work with other people."
> *Sally Ride, astronaut*

Conventions/Trade Shows/Trade Fairs

Select conventions relating to your area of interest. You may have to travel to the nearest large city to attend a convention. The best way to find out about conventions in your field of interest is to ask people in the industry which conventions and shows their companies attend. In addition, the Chamber of Commerce in most cities can provide a schedule of upcoming conventions. You can expect to see an entire floor of an exhibit hall filled with product displays mounted by various companies for their targeted customers. If you visit an exhibitor's booth at the right time, you may meet the sales manager responsible for sales in your city. Most members of top management will be present, enabling you to meet key people. You may have to pay to obtain entry into the convention or trade show. Sometimes there is a fee for a visitor's pass or browser badge, but often admission is free.

If you have difficulty finding a visitor's pass or if the cost is prohibitive, you may want to investigate other strategies for gaining admittance. One job-seeker I interviewed, Karen, wanted to explore the possibility of going into medical or pharmaceutical sales. She worked in the sales and reservation office of an airline and wanted to switch industries. She got a contact in the field to invite her to a medical convention.

"When we arrived at the convention center," she said, "we found that the visitor's badges were fifty dollars each to gain entry. My friend had already received one through another contact. We started trying to figure out how to get me in for free, too. Hoping to find a badge that had been dropped or lost, I scoured the conventional hall floor, the restaurant, the shuttle buses that bring attendees from their hotels to the convention center—even the floor of the bathroom.

"After a futile, thirty- to forty-five-minute search, we were feeling discouraged, and I was about to leave. My friend implored me to wait a few more minutes. She looked around and recognized a gentleman at a pay phone as the product manager for a company that manufactures medical sutures. She walked up to him, smiled, introduced herself, and explained that I needed a pass to gain admittance to the convention so that I could look for a sales position. Two minutes later, we had a visitor's badge. My friend even introduced me to the manager as we accepted the badge. Later, I went back to his booth to thank him for his generosity—and to give him a copy of my resume!"

If, like Karen, you find it difficult to gain entry to the convention and if you can't afford a pass, find out the names of some exhibitors and call in advance to ask whether you can volunteer your services at the convention. Perhaps you could help a company set up or break down its display (if the company doesn't already use a professional service) or occasionally companies use models to demonstrate their equipment. This may limit your ability to circulate, but it is better than not going at all. Other times, there may be no entry fee. Just walk right in and start making contacts. If you absolutely cannot gain entry to the convention floor, don't despair. One candidate stood outside the entrance of the exhibit hall making contacts with reps and managers as they arrived. Your ability to walk on to the convention floor will depend on the industry, the convention, and your ingenuity.

"Eighty percent of success is showing up."
Woody Allen

Whenever you go someplace where there is a chance for you to meet sales contacts, always bring your resume and a cover letter. At conventions, the people you hope to make contact with may often be occupied with customers. They may not have time to talk to you for long, but they should at least have time for you to introduce yourself and hand them a resume and cover letter that will help them remember you later. The letter should explain that you are attending the meeting in an effort to make contacts for full- or part-time positions or internships. Make sure you do not interrupt anyone who is engaged in speaking with a customer or potential customer. It is not uncommon to attend a convention or trade show with more than twenty thousand attendees milling about. During a three-day show, exhibitors may talk to hundreds of people, introducing products, making contacts, and prospecting—as well as doing some hard selling. The last thing they want is to be interrupted by someone when they are in the middle of making a presentation to a prospect. A good time to visit the booths is when the attendees are in sessions or lectures. Try not to go during break time when the attendees are visiting the booths. Check to see when the breaks are scheduled, and plan your visits around them.

Think carefully about your goals before going to one of these shows. A few weeks before the convention, target companies you know will be exhibiting by calling the companies to ask for names of reps and managers who will be attending and by writing several letters to national sales managers of exhibiting companies. In the letters, inform them that you will be attending the upcoming convention, that you are looking to make a career move, and that you would like to meet with them at their booth should they have some spare time during the show. At the show, stop by each booth when the manager is free. This way you may win a few minutes of quality

Networking in the Apparel Industry

While I was doing research for this book, I took a shot at getting into the Apparel Mart in Dallas. How? I called one of the sports apparel shoe companies, found out the sales rep's name and phone number, then called the rep and pretended I was looking to switch from medical sales to sports apparel sales. It just so happened that the rep was planning to hire a sub rep for part of her territory. I asked her if she was going to be in the company's showroom at the market. She said she was and suggested that we meet there.

That Saturday, I went to the Mart, located her showroom, and was given a visitor's badge at the reception area. At the registration desk I explained that I had an interview scheduled with the sales rep in her showroom. The registration clerk gave me the showroom guide, which was just like the ones produced for other conventions. The guide contained the layout of the showrooms, names of the clothing manufacturers and lines, and the sales reps' names and numbers. Not only did I meet with that rep, but I was also able to meet with several others.

In addition, I encountered a sales rep who represented one of my favorite lines of cotton casual sportswear. She had a slow period during which no one else was in the showroom. She and I started chatting and I asked her how she became the sales rep for this line. She said she had worked in the buyer's office of a department store. The owner of the cotton line used to come in to sell to the buyers. She kept asking him to let her work his showroom during market, if he needed assistance, and eventually, he did. Then, when the line expanded, he gave her the job of representing the territory. She was only a few years out of college and making around $50,000 a year. Also, she was given the company's great cotton sportswear outfits to wear, so she did not have to buy clothes! For someone wanting to break into apparel sales, she would have been an excellent contact. Meeting her was not only easy, but fun!

time with the manager to discuss your goals. You'll not only have a great reason to introduce yourself, he may even be expecting you!

A week before the meeting starts, begin trying to obtain a badge by networking with friends and contacts in the industry. An industry contact may be able to put your name on the guest list for her company. Once inside, pick up an Exhibit Guide, which lists the companies and their corresponding booth numbers and which also contains a diagram of the convention center and the show's layout. There is usually a listing of companies by product. To make the most of the time you have at the meeting, highlight the booths that are must-sees, and mark the booths you would like to visit. Remember, you want to make as many contacts as possible.

Look first, of course, for the locations of those companies to which you have sent letters. Begin walking past their booths, looking for an appropriate time to stop by. The occupants of the booths may stay busy almost constantly. Just circle around several times until there is a lull. Spot the national sales managers or particular reps by looking for titles on name badges. When one candidate, Linda, attended her first sales convention, one manager, whom she had written to in advance, remembered who she was when he saw her name badge. "He looked at my name and said, 'Hello Linda, I received your letter and resume just days ago. I see you did stop by when I was not busy.' He realized that I had been walking by the booth but did not interrupt him while he was talking to customers."

> "Be prepared. You never get a second chance to make a good first impression."
>
> *Life's Little Instruction Book*

When you make a contact at a convention, always request literature on the company's products and ask for a business card. You may want to jot a note on the back of the

Making Contact at Conventions

Again, utilize your talents in volunteering. While I was doing research for this book, I ended up at the "Fitness Idea Convention," produced by the International Association of Fitness Professionals (IDEA). At their toll-free number, 800-999-4332, I found out the dates and other information about the upcoming event.

Through the Chamber of Commerce, I found out that the IDEA meeting was to be held in New Orleans. Through a local paper, I learned that it was to be held at the convention center. This particular convention was open to the public, so that was added reason for me to attend. I did not have to pay for a browser's badge to get in the door. Not only did I obtain information on how to find a sales position in the sports apparel field, but I found some great bargains on aerobic clothes for myself.

When I walked in the door and started browsing, I suddenly wished that my mentor had specialized in this field. My life might have taken a different path, but it sure would have been fun! More than 350 booths displayed the latest fitness technology, products, and information.

The Nike exhibit was exciting. Aerobics instructors were performing step classes to rap music. Booths were crowded with trainers and instructors talking to sales reps. Reps were busy presenting information about their products. Attendees were buying clothes and shoes and receiving professional discounts.

As I walked around, I felt really out of place. I had on a designer, navy blue pin-striped suit. Instead of business attire, I should have worn something a little more casual. *Remember, you have to dress the part for the industry that you target.* Most of those in attendance wore aerobics clothes, warm-up suits, shorts, and leggings.

In spite of my self-consciousness, I approached the Nike booth, and asked to speak with a local sales rep. I spoke with one of the Nike reps and discovered there were two open sales positions, one in New Orleans and another one somewhere else in Louisiana. I asked the rep for her card and information about getting in touch with the sales manager. She was nice and gave me a lot of information on how to make contact with the company. Had I wanted to, I could have contacted her later on and elicited more information on the job openings.

Next, I headed down the exhibit hall to the aerobic clothes section. I bought several outfits and then asked to see the manager or owner of the company whose outfit I had purchased. I asked each one of them how they hired sales reps. These were the responses: We hire reps who have some experience or who are currently representing other lines. Our reps are independent and carry as many as ten lines. When the reps become too busy to handle it all by themselves, they may hire sub reps to help them with large territories.

These reps work on straight commission and pay all of their own expenses. Each person I spoke with took my resume and gave me his business card. The clothing lines I looked at were the same lines of aerobic clothes I had been buying from department stores and sports and health clubs for years.

All of these companies participated in this convention. You could walk right up and make face to face contact with reps from any one of them. Had I known this when I was in college, I would have attended these shows, met some of the reps and tried to become a sub rep for a couple of lines. Not only would I have gained sales experience, I would have had great discounts on clothes and made money selling. I discovered through questioning the company representatives that sports apparel/goods companies locate reps by asking buyers at department stores, sporting goods outlets, and health clubs for recommendations. They also hire reps away from these places. The reps are generally college graduates who have worked in stores through college and who network with the sales reps as they come into the stores.

The reps I saw at this convention were young, attractive, athletic adults, and they looked as though they were having a blast. In addition to attending this convention, I have frequented ski equipment and apparel conventions, gone to fashion apparel marts during market week. The same criteria that apply to one industry apply to the other. Employers look within the industry, among the customer base, (in the stores) and hire sub reps when their territories become too large to handle. Much hiring is through word of mouth, so it helps to be in the limelight to get noticed.

You can pick and choose what you want to do to gain experience and have fun doing it. Be creative. Call organizations like IDEA and ask them to help you make contact with companies within their industry and to tell you where the next convention is being held. Send letters and offer to volunteer—setting up for the meeting, breaking down displays, anything you can do to get your big toe in the door—just to make contacts with the companies. As you make contacts with the companies or sales reps, be alert to other tasks you can help them with. A company may welcome your offer to volunteer at a fashion market or trade show as a runner, model, or greeter, in exchange for providing you with information and a little experience. Once you've made contact with professionals in your industry of choice, you'll be on your way!

business card concerning your conversation, possible openings, or a comment that the person made. If you meet a manager, try to make sure you get his fax number, mailing address, and telephone or voice mail number, so you can call or write a follow-up letter. A voice mail number or e-mail address allows you to stay in contact: Every three to six months you can leave a polite, "Hello, I am still looking for a sales position" message.

When the convention concludes, take all of the cards you have gathered and organize them so you can start sending follow-up letters. A contact may not have had any positions open that day, but she may in the future. Always send another copy of your resume and cover letter with your follow-up letter. The person you spoke with may have left your resume in the booth, lost it, or misplaced it. Some conventions become resume swap meets, and yours could have been moved to the bottom of the pile.

GROCERY STORES

The best way to meet sales reps for packaged consumer goods is through your local supermarket. Sales reps are usually there early in the morning or on a specific day of the week to call on the store manager. Ask the store manager to tell you what day the representatives will be in the store. Also, you can find out if any store sets are scheduled. Arrange your schedule so you can be at the store on those days.

STORE SETS

Store sets provide an opportunity to meet several reps at one time. Reps frequently have to go into a store—particularly in large grocery store chains such as Delchamps and Albertsons—to restock products. The reps work late at night or during the day, depending on when the store sets are scheduled. Frequently, stores are closed to customers during the process because moving masses of merchandise on and off shelves and "resetting" them can become messy.

Store sets also offer an opportunity to pinpoint available consumer sales positions. The experience of meeting actual reps in the field and the connections you make from it will pay off. If the store set is open to reps only, try another approach. As the reps pull up in front of the store to unload supplies and displays from their trunks, offer to assist by carrying in their displays or briefcases. This will enhance the possibility of accompanying them into the store.

National Chain Headquarters/ Local Distribution Centers

You can also locate consumer sales reps and their managers at major chain store headquarters and distribution centers. Generally, these reps are called national account managers. These managers call on the buyers of nationally distributed products. One job-seeker I knew went to the headquarters of A&P grocery stores in New Orleans looking to make contacts with sales reps. When the account managers and divisional or regional managers would drive into the parking lot, he would catch them in the lobby of the building as they approached the reception area. If they had to wait to see the buyer, he would talk to them and question them. There he learned what managers do at the national level. Generally, the managers he met were former reps who had been promoted to national account managers. They would make presentations to the buyers concerning volume discounts, special promotions, seasonal advertisements, new products, and more. Often, these reps knew about open positions, and how to contact the managers.

Store Openings

Store openings, though infrequent, are fertile ground for meeting sales reps. Keep an eye out for new stores being built. Close to opening day, find out when the reps will be arriving to set the store. On Grand Opening Day, there are always reps in the stores.

Food Shows

Many of the large supermarket chains hold food shows for their store managers, inviting the packaged goods companies to display their wares. Generally, these food shows are held once a year, though it depends on the chain. These shows are similar to trade conventions and are held for the benefit of the exhibitors and store managers. They usually take place in large cities at different times of the year. Ask the store managers of your local grocery stores when they hold their food shows. There are major national and international food fairs held in cities such as Chicago and San Francisco. The largest food show in the world is the Food Marketing Institute (FMI) show held annually in Chicago. The phone number in Washington, D.C., is 202-452-8444, for dates and times for this meeting.

Consumer companies are required to set up their booths in advance of the meetings, which are typically held at hotels or convention centers. The strategy of offering to lend a hand is always effective. Again, you might try to arrange to attend by obtaining a badge from one of the companies or from a friend you have made through hanging out with the sales reps.

Drug Stores

The different types of reps who call on drug stores range from pharmaceutical reps for both over-the-counter and prescription drugs, cosmetic reps, consumer goods reps, and others.

WHOLESALE STORES — WAL-MART/K-MART

All stores that buy products from consumer companies are serviced and merchandised by sales representatives from the companies. The wide range of products available at discount stores and wholesalers makes them a great place to meet reps from a variety of industries.

HOSPITALS

Hospital lobbies afford opportunities to make contact with reps in the medical or pharmaceutical sales field. Reps will often be on the phone. You can identify a sales contact by looking for those wearing business attire—men and women in suits carrying briefcases.

Also, check out hospital restaurants, parking lots, and pharmacies. The reps sport briefcases containing medical samples, or they pull carts on rollers. Since most medical reps start in the hospital purchasing office, try to make contacts there. Remember, though, you are in a hospital. Most hospitals don't like people wandering through the halls, so follow protocol and behave professionally. Stay out of operating rooms and other restricted areas.

Don't be obnoxious or you'll be escorted to the door by security. Keep in mind that the reps are there on business, not there to answer your fifty questions on how to find a sales position. If they are busy, ask for a card and make contact later. Or if they have time available, offer to buy them a cup of coffee in the coffee shop. But be prepared to be told, "I do not have time to talk." Also, many reps may be protective of their know-how and refuse to share it. Just remember, although you may obtain your information piecemeal, in the end you will get what you need. Be patient—and persistent.

HOTELS/RESORTS

To find sales managers and sales reps as they travel their territories, hold sales meetings, and even conduct interviews, try hotels. Many sales reps have had more interviews in the lobbies, restaurants, and rooms of hotels than they have had vacations in them. The best opportunities are at airport hotels, downtown hotels, or hotels located near convention halls.

Some managers utilize hotels to interview candidates for open sales territories. The front desk staff always knows which companies are interviewing, because the candidates will come in and inquire at the front desk for the manager and company. It's not uncommon to meet managers in hotel coffee shops as they review resumes before starting a day of interviews.

Some companies hold divisional, regional, or national sales meetings in large city hotels or resorts. Most hotels will list information on TV screens, marquees, and bulletin boards—including schedules for company meetings and the rooms in which they will be held. Now, please do not plan to crash the company cocktail party or reception, but you could show up in the morning and mill around outside in the hall until break time.

During the break, ask one of the reps to point out a sales manager. Then, when he is unoccupied, walk over and introduce yourself. One way to lead in is to hand him your resume with a cover letter explaining that you knew their meeting was being held at this hotel and that you would like to interview for a sales position.

AIRPORTS

In addition to hotels, sales managers often interview candidates for sales positions in airports. American Airlines' Admirals Club and Delta Crown Rooms are two of the most common sites for interviews. Managers may reserve certain rooms at airports for interviewing potential sales candidates in major hub cities like Dallas, Chicago, Los Angeles, New Orleans. Use your connections to find out who is interviewing and when.

SPORTING GOOD STORES/SPORTS APPAREL MARKET

One job-seeker, an avid skier, was interested in breaking into the sporting goods industry as a sales rep. On a trip to a local ski store, he picked up a catalog for a new line of skis and asked the owner of the store a couple of questions. First, he asked who the rep for the ski company was and where the person was located. He eventually managed to contact her in Denver. She confirmed what he had already heard about the ski industry—that the reps stay in it for a long time. (Indeed, ski industry reps stay with their companies longer than in any other field I've investi-

"Ask, and it shall be given; seek, and ye shall find; knock, and it shall be opened unto you."

Matthew 7:7

gated.) She also mentioned that reps often hired sub reps and that they found them through ski shops or by word of mouth. When she told him she needed a model for a show in his home city, it occurred to him that modeling would be a great way to meet all the reps from the different ski companies. He later wrote the Denver rep a letter offering his services as a model and expressing his interest in finding a sales job in the field. He also included a picture of himself along with his resume.

If you are interested in contacting sporting goods and apparel sales reps in the ski industry, look in the back of *Ski* magazine. You will find a list of all the ski companies and their telephone numbers. By using the phone number listed in the back of the magazine, you can contact the sales representatives through the company's customer service department.

Making the contact is not hard, but this industry is a tough one to break into. You have to really want to get in. Be willing to start at the bottom, work hard, and make contact after contact. There are a couple of different shows (one major ski goods market is held in Las Vegas). Ask the companies which ones they attend.

Toastmasters/Clubs/Organizations

One sales rep stressed how much her social connections and contacts helped her land her job. She served on a fundraising committee for the local museum, the Chamber of Commerce, and several other high profile organizations. Why? Because she viewed members of those organizations as potential customers. Look into making contacts through breakfast meetings or networking meetings in your city. Many sales reps join such clubs and attend the seminars that they put on just to make contacts.

Health Clubs

Most sales reps work out—not all, but most. Have you noticed that sales reps are generally in shape? Appearance and stamina are important to their line of work. Sales managers observe everything. Successful job candidates land positions not only because they have the background, experience, and contacts, but because of their presence. Working out gives you confidence in the way you carry yourself. If you are fit, you are in shape, you feel good, and it shows. Not all reps are in shape, but the majority seem to be. It certainly can't hurt!

> "No man knows what he can do until he tries."
>
> *Syrius Publilius*

Your local gym is a great place to meet other reps. Encountering them under these circumstances will allow you a good thirty minutes or so to pry out of them lots of answers and to get in shape at the same time. When you meet reps at the health club, make friends with them and offer to help out in exchange for their imparting a little knowledge and experience. You never know when one of your workout buddies will decide to leave his position and recommend you as a replacement!

3

Talking to Contacts:
Getting Useful Information

IN CHAPTER TWO, YOU LEARNED HOW TO BE AN EXPERT sleuth who, like Columbo zeroing in on a murder suspect, uncovers the hideouts of target sales managers and reps. You've also mastered how to "case" parking lots, conventions, office buildings, or apparel markets to locate as many contacts as possible. The contacts will be professionals who have been reps or managers trained by the companies where you want to find positions. Now you must learn to project the right impression when making these initial contacts. What do you say to these people to gain the vital "audition time" you need? You must also learn how to solicit useful information from these contacts once you have their attention—information about internship programs, open positions, or any other beneficial opportunities your contact may be aware of. By developing contacts with people directly associated with your field of interest, you learn

> "Every man I meet is in some way my superior and I can learn from him."
>
> *Ralph Waldo Emerson*

35

not only what positions are available, but also such valuable information such as *why* the positions are open and who to contact concerning the positions.

If by good fortune you make contact with a sales manager with an open territory, you will be instantly scrutinized by this potential employer. Basically, this may be your first interview with a manager and possibly your last if you aren't properly prepared. But if you know the right buzz words and can put your best foot forward during this unplanned event, you could be called in for a formal interview or possibly made a job offer. If not prepared, you're in jeopardy of leaving your contact with an unfavorable first impression—and of losing your chance to ever make a second.

BE PREPARED

If you start talking to people around you and ask what they do, you will be amazed how many sales people are out there. An opportunity to make contact with one of them could arise at any time. You may be able to make contacts using the methods in Chapter Two, but don't limit yourself! The man dressed in a jogging suit who is behind you in the grocery store checkout line may be the National Sales Manger or division sales manager of a Fortune 500 company. Hopefully, the line will be long and the checker will be slow so you will have the time to let him know a little about you and your ambition. He may be the key to meeting your goal of a sales position.

> "The secret of success is to be ready for opportunity when it comes."
>
> *Benjamin Disraeli*

Meeting people in such situations gives you the opportunity to talk with them while their guard is down, which sometimes makes it easier to elicit information. It could happen any time, any place.

36

You must constantly be as prepared to make a contact as you would be to go on an interview. Suppose you meet a rep calling on a store, but she explains to you that this isn't actually her territory. The regular sales rep has just left the position, and she is covering the territory while her manager interviews people to fill the position. Such scenarios happen every day, but if you are not in the line of action you will never be able to take advantage of them. But how do you establish solid contact with someone who is a total stranger?

INITIATING CONVERSATION

The following scenario is one approach you could use when meeting sales reps or managers. This is just an example and should be adapted to fit the situation when you actually meet a sales rep or manager. For now, however, imagine you are on the pay phone in the lobby of a hotel. (Perhaps you're on vacation or you've heard that reps frequently stay at this hotel.) Next to you is a man in a suit who is also on the phone. You overhear him talking to a customer about scheduling an appointment to show him a new line of drugs from a pharmaceutical company.

Once he is off the phone, you might smile and say something like, "Hi, you must be a sales rep with a pharmaceutical company." He responds, "Yes, I am." Introduce yourself and tell him you are currently looking for a position in pharmaceutical sales. "I know that reps like yourself often hear about open positions before most other people do and that recruiters call you to try to woo you away for other positions. Do you know of any companies in the industry who have open positions?" If he doesn't know of any sales rep positions available, ask about internships and flex or part time opportunities.

Or rather than asking him for information on job openings, try picking his brain for information about his industry, company, and position. If you're nervous, start off with something innocuous like,

"Hi, I noticed your unique briefcase, I've never seen one like that before. Where did you find it? Are you a sales rep? What do you like about selling? Why did you choose to work for your present company? What are some of the current trends in your industry? How is your company better than your competition?"

If you happen to run into a sales manager that conducts interviews for his company, be sure to give him the best impression possible of your experience and abilities. Introduce yourself and say, "I am looking for a sales position. Last week I rode in the field with a pharmaceutical sales rep in exchange for helping him organize his samples, typing a couple of reports, and assisting him while he was putting on a luncheon."

Now you have this manager's attention. You could tell him you are looking for a position in sales and wanted to make contacts and gain some experience at the same time. Then you can question him about open positions and follow up with a copy of your resume.

> "Good fortune is what happens when opportunity meets with preparation."
>
> Thomas Edison

Use these as examples and develop introductions that you're comfortable using. Practice them on friends and in front of the mirror. Once you put them into practice they will become natural over time. You'll learn to adapt them to the different types of people you meet. Looking for a sales job is like looking for a husband or wife—you only need one. And that could come from the next contact you make!

CREATING MEANINGFUL DIALOGUE

Once you have opened a conversation with a manager or rep, it's important to move the discussion along quickly. Your contact will be busy and may not have time to talk for long. On the other hand, you want to get as much information from them as you can. If you are prepared enough to sound knowledgeable and engaging, and if you are polite, respectful, and genuinely curious, the contact may be happy to take the time to talk with you. Don't let the conversation lag or fly off on a tangent. Ask the rep or manager open-ended questions, allowing him to talk as long as they wish. The longer he talks, the more information you'll receive. Find out as much as you can about his knowledge of the business, his perception of the market, his individual insight into the sales process, as well as current information on his specific products and his products' competitors. In other words, pick your contact's brain to find out information that you need to become a well-informed job candidate. Asking questions, both open-ended and pointed, will allow you to stay informed not only about sales in general, but also about issues specific to individual industries. As you converse with contacts, you will be surprised at how quickly you will sound like you know what you are talking about.

To solve a problem, ask the person who performs the task for the solution.

Here's a list of questions you can ask to facilitate conversation with your contact. They will also help you learn more about the industry you want to work in, what a sales job entails, and how other reps found their positions. Again, these are only examples, and as you read through the

"Who knows the job better than the man close to it?"

Kimsy Mann, chairman, Blue Bell

chapters and gain more experience, you should add to it and eventually make up a list of questions of your own.

- How did you land your first sales position?
- Who are you working for?
- If you had to do it all over again, what would you do differently?

39

- What are the most difficult questions you were ever asked on an interview? How did you respond?
- What do managers look for in your industry?
- Do managers in your industry use recruiters?
- Do reps in your industry get referral fees for recommending other sales reps?
- Is your industry growing?
- Do you have a lot of competition?
- Who are your competitors?
- If you could have any sales position, who would you want to work for and why?
- How did you organize your territory?
- Who do you call on?
- How many sales calls do you make in a day?
- How long did it take you to start making your sales numbers?
- How are the reps in your industry paid?
- What should a person applying for entry level position expect for a compensation package?
- How do reps in your industry negotiate for the highest compensation package?
- What have you found to be effective in making sales?
- How do you find open sales positions?
- What is the best part of the job? The worst?
- Do you want to get promoted to management?
- What are sales reps called in your industry? What are the sales managers' titles?
- Do you know of any open positions in the industry?
- Could I call you sometime when you have time and meet you for a cup of coffee to talk about the your industry?
- Do you know of any sub rep positions open?
- Do you know of any companies that offer internships for college students?
- Do you know of any companies that will hire new people with little or no sales experience?

- What conventions, trade shows, or markets are coming up?
- Would you mind if I see a copy of your resume and the cover letter that you used to land your current position?
- What sales courses or seminars have you attended that you feel would be good for an entry-level person?
- What sales books would you recommend?

These examples are generic questions and are not specific to any one industry. Selling surfboards and selling carpet are two very different jobs. They may have some things in common, but there is a wealth of questions you could ask about either one. You should work toward developing a list of questions specific to your industry of interest.

Be bold—that is the only way you will find out anything. The contact may be up for promotion to management and looking for someone to replace him in the field after he moves up. He may have received a call from a recruiter about an open position, or he may have recently met another rep who told him about a friend who had just taken a position at another company.

If the rep seems friendly and responds positively to your questions, then you may want to ask him for a card. Reps may even ask whether you have a resume with you. One rep asked a job-seeker to send her a copy of his resume because she had a friend who did recruiting. Another knew several sales managers who had openings. These are the types of situations you should be working to set up. The more contacts you make, the more chances you have of hitting a bull's eye—a job opening.

CREATE OPPORTUNITIES TO FOLLOW UP

Remember that although an initial conversation with a contact can be tremendously helpful, your ultimate goal is to build this new acquaintance into a relationship you can count on in the future. To establish such a relationship, it's essential to follow up on every initial contact you make. Always try to obtain a business card and ask the contact whether it would be all right to call him in the future. If nothing else, follow up with a note or a phone call thanking the contact for his time and for the valuable information he shared. However, if you're properly prepared, much more can be accomplished with follow-up calls.

One sales rep tells the story of how, while looking for a sales position, she had calling cards like the example shown below made at a print shop with her qualifications on the back, like a mini-resume. Because the cards were small and easy to give to any potential contact, she could keep them with her at all times. First, she would initiate a conversation, and then eventually bring it around to herself, saying, "This is my card, and my qualifications for a sales position are listed on the back. Do you have a card so I can contact you later or send you a copy of my resume?" A contact may not have an open position when you first meet, but he may have a lead within a short period of time. The calling card gets his attention, and you get a reason to contact him at a later date. When making contacts, a card such as this can be just as effective as handing out a resume— and much more convenient.

Megan Falconer
123 Main Street, Dallas, Texas 76543
(555) 123-4567

OBJECTIVE
A position in marketing or sales using my education and experience in the medical field

---

Front

QUALIFICATIONS

More than four years experience as a professional critical care nurse.

Excellent communicator with good human relations skills.

Expertise at interacting with medical professionals at all levels.

Experienced in sales and customer service.

Computer literate with exprience using Windows, Word Perfect, and custom hospital software.

Inside Fold

EDUCATION

Associates Degree in Nursing 1992
Diploma in Fashion Merchandising 1980

CONTINUING EDUCATION

Consultive Selling 1996
Critical Care Internship 1993

PROFESSIONAL AFFILATIONS

National Association Female Executives

Back

The resume card can be used as a temporary resume that can be carried in a purse or a wallet and handed out to contacts. The card should contain an overview of your resume and highlight your greatest accomplishments. It is an attention-grabbing teaser that hopefully will have your contacts anxiously awaiting your resume. This is one more way that you can stand out from other candidates when seeking a career in sales. The purpose of the card is threefold:

- It is small enough to always have one ready to hand to a contact.
- It is different from what other candidates will hand out.
- It makes you look more creative, organized, and well-prepared than other candidates.

Collect the contact's card and write notes on the back regarding your conversation. If he has an immediate opening, then send your resume as soon as possible. If not, in a week or two, send a brief note reminding him of your encounter, with a copy of your resume as you promised. Also, a follow-up call is a perfect time to ask your contact for referrals. He may not know of a position himself, but he may know several people you could contact for more information.

Making follow-up calls or contacting referrals by phone is more intrusive than sending a note or striking up a conversation in person. Remember that your contacts are very busy, and they may not appreciate the interruption. Therefore, when using the phone to talk to contacts, it is essential to observe the following rules:

- Ask whether your contact has a few moments to speak with you.
- If he says no, or if he hesitates, ask whether you could call back at a more convenient time.
- If he is willing to speak with you, make your point quickly and concisely.
- Use proper English diction and grammar.
- Be courteous, organized, and professional.

The Principle of Mutual Benefits

Making contacts is not a predatory activity. At its best, it creates relationships that are beneficial for all concerned. As you ask your contact for information during your initial meeting or during follow-up calls, always offer to do something in return, like organizing his samples, typing a couple of reports, or assisting him in some simple task. This will enhance the possibility of his keeping an eye open for you. Furthermore, proposing a working relationship such as this is an ideal way to develop and strengthen your contact.

One sales rep for a shoe company line was asked the following question:

"If I knew someone looking for sales job, say a student or career changer, and he wanted to learn how to get a job in the shoe industry, would you let him ride with you for a day or so in the field to observe you on a day-to-day basis?"

He replied,

"I would have to think about it, but probably no."

Then the question was posed another way:

"I have a candidate who is dying to learn how to get into your industry. He is willing to help you do your paperwork, type your past-due reports, help you straighten out your samples, help you at market as a greeter, or even try to help you sell at market if you teach him how to present to the buyers."

He then replied,

"That's hard to turn down."

As you will see in Chapter Eight, part of the job is paperwork. Weekly or monthly reports and sales projections all need to be neatly typed. Also, many reps have to write follow-up letters to customers. If you can type or are adept at writing, this may be a lead-in with a sales rep. If you have a week off before Christmas, you might offer to send his Christmas cards to his customers or deliver presents during the holidays. Then explain that in exchange, you would like to ride with him for a couple of days during your vacation.

When you go with him each day, don't forget to watch how he sells the product to customers. Take note of how he dresses, how he converses, and how he meets customers. You will get a firsthand feel for the field and be able to judge if this is the type of work you would like to do. This will come in handy when you are interviewing, because you can say that you've ridden in the field with sales reps to verify that this was something that suited your personality and fell in line with your skills. Then you will know that you are comfortable in the environment and will feel that you can be effective. Remember to follow up with a thank-you letter outlining the activities and things you learned. Then you have something to put in your Atta-Way File.

Forming a working relationship with a rep is also a wonderful way to meet other contacts and pinpoint open positions. While you are working with the rep, you may run into other reps. Be prepared to introduce yourself and explain what you are doing. Collect their business cards and hand out your resume cards.

MAKING CONTACT WITH RECRUITERS

Recruiters are another valuable contact source for the job-seeker. Call and meet with at least two or three professional recruiters. There are books available that list names and phone numbers (see list below), or better yet, ask one of the contacts you make to give you a name of a good recruiter—especially anyone who calls him with good positions.

BOOKS OF RECRUITERS

- *The Directory of Executive Recruiters*. James Kennedy. (Kennedy Information.)
- *Guide to Executive Recruiters*. Michael Betrus. (McGraw-Hill, Inc.)
- *The Best Directory of Recruiters*. (Grove Publishing.)

Since a recruiter's job is to recruit sales reps who have gained experience from their entry-level positions and place them in better positions with other companies, he has information that you will want to know. You may not have the experience to fill the positions the recruiter is trying to fill, but you *do* want find out about the entry-level positions that are being vacated by the reps the recruiter talks to. When contacting a recruiter, it is important to remember that even though you may not be able to fill one of the positions the recruiter is concerned with, you still have something to offer. Plan ahead, so that when a recruiter says he can't help you find a job because you don't have enough experience, you can counter that with a version of the mutual benefits principle. Over the course of your job search, you've been making contacts with reps with two to three years of sales experience. You have even collected their business cards and other information—information that the recruiter wants. Offer to make a trade—your information about experienced sales reps in exchange for solid leads on entry-level job opportunities.

When you get contacts from the recruiter, call the sales rep who's leaving a position and ask him to put you in contact with his manager. Even though the rep is leaving, he may have a good relationship with his manager. In fact, many departing reps want to help out their managers by suggesting a replacement. This is your opportunity to have the rep hand your resume to the manager personally.

Here's an example of how this can work: A medical recruiter may

47

have a job order for an entry-level medical position. Many medical companies like to recruit away from the consumer or copier industry, because these entry-level reps have been well trained at corporations like Procter & Gamble, Johnson Wax, or Xerox. Therefore, if the recruiter takes the Procter & Gamble rep and places them at entry-level with a medical company, the Procter & Gamble position is now open. The recruiter has nothing to gain by not telling you about the open position, because he only works in the medical field.

What is important about this situation is that you have transformed a recruiter's objection about your lack of experience into an opportunity he cannot say no to. You are offering to give him candidates' names and phone numbers in exchange for information about open entry-level positions. The company that now has an open position is not likely to hire the recruiter to replace the candidate he took from them, so the recruiter usually has no further interest in that position.

Although it seems unethical, a recruiter may take one candidate from one company and place him with another. The recruiter then calls the manager of the first company to pick up the job order for the now open entry-level position. You will have to use your best judgment about which recruiters you deal with.

Another angle you may use with the recruiter is that, while you are making contacts, you may find open positions that you are not qualified to fill. You could offer information about these positions to the recruiter. Recruiters usually have limited opportunities to get out of the office. They mostly depend on reps to tell them what is going on in the industry, and they work from tips and referrals to find open positions.

Make friends with the recruiters and follow up with them often. Set a pattern of calling them every few weeks just to check in. Don't keep giving them information if they never give you anything in return. Find a recruiter who will give you leads on entry-level positions in return for your information.

4

Getting Your Foot in the Door: Creating Opportunities for Experience

IDEALLY, YOU MUST APPEAR TO BE A POTENTIAL producer trained in selling and experienced in the field to demonstrate you are a low risk and can promise financial return to a company. If you are currently a candidate who requires professional sales and field training, one who will deplete a company's funds and resources rather than produce income immediately, you are a higher risk candidate.

Think of hiring from an employer's perspective. Companies look for a person with something to offer—sales experience, knowledge of the industry, familiarity with the customer base or product. Although some companies have training programs for inexperienced reps, most are not interested in an interviewee saying, "Teach me." It costs money and time to train a sales rep and to transform him into a productive asset.

> "You cannot create experience; you must undergo it."
>
> *Albert Camus, French philosopher and writer*

49

I WANNA BE A SALES REP!

To prepare for an interview you must be able to answer the question, "What can I do for this company?" You must find the answer to that question through experience. You need to define how you are going to create experience either from options listed in this chapter, or through your own ingenuity. While gaining experience, it is vital that you document every single thing you do, and every person you come into contact with. Your objective, beginning now, is to build this documentation of your experience into a substantial presentation. Keep several files or a file box of everything you do. You can always go back later and organize the box of papers.

We can't start at the top, but when we do get there, we arrive with sales and field experience and appreciation for the job. Using each experience as a stepping stone to land that first sales position will put you ahead of the other candidates.

> "You are your first product, so positioning yourself in the market as an individual is extremely important."
>
> Portia Isaacson,
> founder,
> Future Computing
> Management

Experience is what makes you into a marketable product. Yes, you are the product that you must sell to a prospective employer. The sales department of a company consists of sales managers, vice presidents of sales, national sales managers, and sometimes international sales managers. These people view your credentials and skills as a "product." You have to sell yourself in an interview as a potential producer. You also have to have enough confidence in yourself to market and present yourself in an interview in a positive light. Experience provides you with the knowledge and confidence necessary to land a job.

THE JOB-SEEKER'S DILEMMA

The common denominator among job-seekers asking for advice is that they lack experience in their field of interest. Even those who may already have experience in sales may lack experience selling within a particular industry.

If you lack experience like most first-time candidates do, you can get around the "no-experience dilemma" by using creativity and ambition to create experience. Bear in mind that the most common reason a candidate is turned down for a sales position is lack of sales experience. The question is, what is meant by lack of experience? It may not always be what it seems. It may actually be inexperience with interviewing for a sales position, with anticipating a sales manager's questions, or with applying current job experience to skills needed for a sales job. Just as important as sales experience is the ability to explain to a sales manager the steps you've taken to train yourself and to demonstrate how creative and ambitious you are.

A plan keeps your efforts going in the right direction.

Most candidates don't understand the importance of using their creativity and ambition to win the position over more experienced candidates. Having a plan of action for demonstrating these qualities to a sales manager on a resume or in an interview is essential. Experienced sales reps are often too confident in an interviewing situation and don't prepare as well as they should. They think, "I'm a shoo-in for this position because I have three years experience and an excellent track record." An air of cockiness can be dangerous. Many sales managers choose the less experienced candidate because he portrays himself as a self-starter who is determined, tenacious, ambitious, and enthusiastic. The following suggestions will help you become prepared to emphasize these qualities and gain the edge over the more experienced candidate.

> "What's the use of running if you're not on the right road?"
>
> *German proverb*

IT TAKES TIME

How much time do you have available to prepare yourself for a sales rep position? One, two, three days a week? Maybe you have only weekends or just a few hours a week. The amount of time you can devote to developing your credentials will be determined by your willingness to balance your schedule in order to carve out time. Think about evenings, weekends, holidays, and vacations. As you proceed through this book, earmark one, two, or maybe three activities that would fit into your schedule. Then make a schedule—and stick to it. Remember, it is *your* schedule. The more time you invest, the faster you will reach your goal.

> "People who make the worst use of their time are the same ones who complain that there is never enough time."
>
> *Anonymous*

Developing sales experience can be a full-time job. But if you could start selling on the side while continuing your day job or your degree, for example, then by the time you start interviewing, you will be able to demonstrate sales experience.

If you are not currently in school or have graduated, you may have to create your own internship to gain the necessary experience. Remember, you are training yourself to be a sales rep, and you must be willing to use all of the methods and materials you can get your hands on. You must show determination to learn and be the best you can be—even without a secured job. This will make an impact on a future employer. Many people give up their job search because the demands become too much, but that is exactly when they should stick it out.

> "A determined person is one who, when he gets to the end of his rope, ties a knot and hangs on."
>
> *Joe L. Griffith*

In the next few pages appear stories collected from interviews with sales reps. These stories are about real life situations that helped these reps find positions. Just like the story of the manager on the plane and how I found my first position, these stories are about how other job candidates succeeded by working in professional internships or by creating their own. Remember, previous experience is not limited to paid positions. Volunteering will put you right where the action is, and will let a potential employer know you have hands-on practice in the field. You'll also find advice on how to find existing internships or how to create new ones.

FINDING INTERNSHIPS

Internships are perhaps the best possible way to gain experience in the sales field. By learning firsthand the tasks faced daily by a sales rep, you can learn far more than you ever could by reading a book or by taking a college course or a sales seminar. In addition, the benefits of working directly with other people in the field are immeasurable. What better way to meet recruiters, managers, and sales reps who could assist you in the future as you search for a full-time sales position? Although internships may not always pay well—if at all—they provide a good way for a job-seeker to get her foot in the door part time, enabling her to get the

> "In the business world, everyone is paid in two coins: cash and experience. Take the experience first, the cash will come later."
>
> Harold Geneen, CEO
> IT&T, Managing.
> (Doubleday)

experience she needs to land a sales job while retaining her old job or continuing her degree. The following is a description of a sales internship in the fashion industry. It should give you an idea not only of what you can expect from a typical sales internship, but also of the tangible benefits experience as an intern can offer. A sales representative who worked for an apparel corporation in New York provided the following outline of an internship the company had developed, which required twenty hours per week. Although it was a nonpaying post, it covered business expenses and offered perks.

The job requirements for Junior Retail Sales Coordinator Intern were as follows:

- Senior class standing or one year till degree completion.
- 3.5 GPA Fashion Institute or 3.0-3.5 GPA major accredited four-year university.
- Work a minimum of fifteen to twenty hours per week.
- Work a minimum of three days per week.
- Nonpaying with perks.
- BA or BS degree in fields directly related to business, marketing, liberal arts, or fashion merchandising.

Job Perks:
- Two outfits per season (e.g., jacket, blouse, skirt, dress).
- Ability to purchase any product line at wholesale.
- All business-related expenses paid (e.g., parking, mileage) or a weekly expense allowance.
- Opportunity to win a trip to attend and assist in New York Market week.
- As a reward for an excellent performance appraisal, intern will be guaranteed an interview with the company.
- Intern will also develop lasting contacts and build a rapport with store management from all the better specialty retailers and department stores in the nation.

The internships for this apparel company are offered in only a few of the major metropolitan areas across the United States. You must apply by writing an essay, filling out an application, and meeting the above job requirements.

A few months later, the rep who provided this information left her position, having found another opportunity selling a different line. Guess who replaced her? The intern who she had trained interviewed for her position and won the job.

Not many of these kinds of internships are available in the fashion industry, but finding a company you may want to work for (in any industry) and writing a proposal letter is the first step—and the only way to land one of them. But how do you locate companies who sponsor such internships, and what is the best way to approach them?

CAMPUS RESOURCES

One sales rep, a man in his mid twenties who works for Johnson Wax, tells this story about how he landed his first sales job with this impressive company:

> "I got lucky," he said. "A company recruiter was on campus at the college I attended, and I was interviewed for an internship position, which I received. I started the internship and went through the company's training program. Then I was assigned to call on a few accounts. After graduation, I got lucky again, because a position opened and I was interviewed by the manager. With the internship and the training under my belt, I landed the position. Best thing that could ever have happened to me. I was really fortunate, because a lot of my friends do not have jobs."

The path of this young individual's professional life is the exception and not the rule. And his experience is not entirely, as he modestly would like us to think, due to luck. To give him the credit he deserves, we must acknowledge the intiative and ambition he demonstrated by going to speak to the campus recruiter in the first place. Too many students do not show up at their college job fairs and do not take advantage of the valuable internship opportunities available there. Most students, too, do not talk to their campus

55

career counselors until they are ready to graduate. If you are in school, put down this book, go to the phone, and call your campus placement department. Make that first appointment and keep going until you have all the information they can give you.

Some companies, such as General Mills, not only train interns to become sales reps, but they also pay the student. Depending on your curriculum and your school, you might even be eligible to receive college credit for your internship.

In the placement office or library at your college, you will find *The National Directory of Internships*, a book that lists companies that offer internships. Alternatively, you can obtain a copy (for about $26) by writing or calling The National Society for Experimental Education, 3509 Haworth Dr., Suite 207, Raleigh, NC 27609; 919-787-3263.

If you are no longer in school, you may still be able to benefit from campus resources such as these. Many career development departments in colleges and universities have listings of job openings and internship opportunities for students who have already graduated. Many also have job lines, bulletin boards, and online services available for alumni to use. These listings may include temporary or part-time positions as well as entry-level sales positions. Also, do not forget traditional avenues such as answering ads in the newspaper and calling recruiters.

Remember there may only be ten internships offered, and 100 students applying for those ten slots. You may have to compete with 99 other students to land one of the ten positions. To make yourself competitive, use the same approach you would take in competing for a full-time sales position. All the information in this book is as relevant to finding and preparing for internship interviews as well as full-time sales position interviews.

CONTACTING REPS

Another avenue you may use to find out which companies have internship programs is to make contacts directly with the sales reps in your field of interest. Most sales reps and managers know about internships within their company and in the industry. You may be lucky enough to find a sales rep who has an intern working under her or who is responsible for field training interns. If this is the case, you should ask how to apply for the next open slot. In addition, always ask how you can get an application, a copy of the requirements for the position, and an outline of the duties, responsibilities, and perks. This information may help you later if you decide to develop your own internship program to present to a company. Creativity in this area has no boundaries. While making contacts always ask about internship programs, entry-level positions, and part-time opportunities. This is a must for gaining experience.

INFORMAL VOLUNTEERING

If you do not land an existing internship position, or if you are not currently in school or have graduated, you may want to consider creating your own internship, whether as a formal position or on a less formal volunteer basis. Offering your services on a volunteer basis to contacts you have made is often a good way to build a rapport with them and to gain valuable experience.

> "Part of networking is realizing what you can do for others."
>
> *John F. Kennedy*

Call a targeted company and ask for information from its Human Resources department, from a product manager, or from a local sales manager. Tell them you are exploring sales rep positions and want to build the desired background before applying. Better yet, if it is a local company, ask if you can come in and talk to them for a few minutes. Chapter Two will help you make face-to-face contact with a potential company employer.

If you connect with a sales manager, say something like, "I am off all summer" (or weekends, evenings, or holidays). "May I help one of your sales reps out in his or her territory?" Ask about conventions and sales meetings. Perhaps the company has taken a booth in a trade show, convention, or product exhibition. Offer to "work the convention," wear the company's volunteer badge, and man the booth with the reps. When the reps need to use the phone or take a break, you'll be there to cover for them. That sure beats leaving the booth empty. Or perhaps you could help with setting the booth up and taking it down. At their sales meetings, they may need a runner or someone to help coordinate the meeting. Volunteer whatever skills you have.

If you make contact with a rep, offer your services to him as well. Sometimes sales reps hire college students to type account profiles and reports. If someone were to approach them and offer to help out for free in exchange for the chance to learn about their job, they'll probably be glad to accommodate you. Act ambitious and be willing to work at whatever task they have for you to do. You could even offer to go to the salesperson's house to help organize his files, trunks, and samples.

If the company you're targeting is a consumer company, offer to help with store sets to gain experience. Who is going to refuse the offer of free labor? It usually takes hours to clear the shelf and replace everything. Sometimes, the reps go in late at night and work until the morning. In situations like these, you may be able to help out for a few hours on a regular basis while still attending classes or holding a job during the day. Always follow up opportunities to help out and to observe sales reps with thank-you letters outlining the activities and procedures you learned. If you've developed a good relationship with the rep or manager, ask him to write a letter recognizing you for assisting in the field. Put a copy of your letter and theirs in your Atta-Way File. This gives you documentation of your experience that you can show to future potential employers.

Expanding your relationship with a rep into an informal internship will give you both invaluable experience and the opportunity to make further contacts. You never know when one of the reps you help may get promoted, quit, or be fired, thereby freeing up an opening. Then again, the rep may have a friend or professional contact in the same industry who's leaving a position to take a better job with another company. Even if your volunteering doesn't lead directly to a job opening, you'll have gained strong resume-building experience that better demonstrates your initiative and ambition than even a formal internship.

CREATING A FORMAL INTERNSHIP

Some companies may be open to someone who is creative and ambitious enough to design and implement a formal internship program. It'll take someone dedicated and persistent to do the background work and organization necessary to create a program. You may also be able to develop an informal volunteering experience into a more formal position.

Start by collecting as much information as you can from every company you have contacted. Most of the companies that offer internships provide a handout that contains a detailed description of the internship. (The fashion industry internship outlined earlier is an example.) Use these descriptions of available internships to design one for yourself. Write one that resembles the samples that you have, but adapt

> "When starting out, don't worry about not having enough money. Limited funds are a blessing, not a curse. Nothing encourages creative thinking in quite the same way."
>
> *Life's Little Instruction Book*

it to the industry you are applying for. Then target a number of companies that you would like to work for and write letters to those that do not offer internships and offer to volunteer a day or two a week as a custom-made intern.

Say, for example, that you have three copies of internship descriptions for consumer companies, but you want to sell computers. Adapt the consumer company's wording to fit a description of an internship for the computer industry. Be resourceful. Maybe you could find a marketing professor or someone in the computer science department of a university to assist you in rewriting the outline or description. Or, call a recruiter in your city to find out whether they have any resumes that contain job descriptions for a computer salesperson or whether they know a sales rep you can contact. Remember that institutions such as hospitals and colleges have information systems departments that buy computers. Call one of the local hospitals and ask the purchasing manager if he can put you in contact with a sales rep. Better yet, call the human resource director of the companies that you are targeting and ask for a job description of a sales rep who works for the company.

> "Many of the best jobs do not really exist until someone is hired for them."
>
> James E. Challenger, president, Challenger, Gery, & Christmas

APPROACHING A COMPANY WITH AN INTERNSHIP PROGRAM PROPOSAL

It is better to ask for too much than too little when making a proposal for a custom internship. For instance, use the same kinds of perks outlined in the fashion industry internship as a set standard. If you want a position, you have to ask for it, and asking for perks is part of the process. The only thing a company can do is turn your proposal down. Too many times novice job-seekers fail to be assertive when asking for a position and perks. In any type of proposal there will be some type of perk or suggested monetary figure. That figure is always negotiable.

Let's say you want to gain experience in apparel sales, but you know there are only two established internships in the entire apparel field and both positions are filled in your area. Start by putting together a proposal to present to other companies in the industry. First try to obtain copies of the duties, requirements, and perks of the two existing ones. Next, write a cover letter expressing your ambitions of working for the company as an intern. With the letter include a proposal with copies of the two existing internships and add what you feel may be missing. Be thorough. Explain that you are going to graduate soon, but were unable to land the two available internship programs in the industry. Explain that you would like to work for the company as a custom-made intern and that you'd be willing to work for a couple of weeks with no perks to allow them to see a sample of your work.

> "The greatest pleasure in life is doing what people say you cannot do."
>
> Walter Bagehot

The best route to presenting your proposal to upper management (who would approve the internship) is to make contact with a sales rep within the company and present it to him first. Having a rep tactfully present your proposal to his manager is far more likely to result in its approval. Not only will the rep be grateful, but also you may be helping him make an impact on his territory and shine brighter in the manager's eyes.

A second alternative is having an important customer of the company present it to the rep or manager. Also, taking your proposal to market and making formal introductions by offering your services may be another avenue.

RETAIL EXPERIENCE

Another great way to make contacts and gain sales experience is through working in retail sales. Many companies hire reps away from department stores, sports and health clubs, and other retail outlets for their products. The reps are often college graduates who have worked in stores through college and who network with the sales reps as they come into the stores. Someone who has worked in a golf and pro shop, for instance, may be hired by the makers of tennis rackets and other products right out of the pro shop.

In almost every industry it is the same: Employers look within the industry among their customer base (at the people in the stores who buy their products to sell to consumers) when they need to hire additional reps or sub reps. Much hiring is through word of mouth, so it helps to be in the limelight to get noticed.

Many fashion apparel sales reps will tell how they were once customers of the company they now rep for. Working in retail is an excellent way to gain valuable experience for a position in apparel sales. You have numerous opportunities to make contact with sales reps, and it allows you to become familiar with the company's product lines and competing lines. One apparel rep tells how she started on the floor in sales and worked her way into a buying position. She was very experienced because she had dealt with the customers of the store, their buying habits, volume of purchases, and merchandising. Having held several positions in that store, she was knowledgeable in all aspects of retail sales.

After she had been in her position for a few years, she felt she had met a ceiling in her position. She started looking into the sales aspect. She wanted to make a career change to apparel sales, so she started networking with the reps and informed them that she was interested in a sales position. One company she was buying from had an opening and recruited her from the store. Companies hire these individuals because they need less training and have the retail experience. In addition, she had experience in buying for a large store, and had previously worked in a boutique ordering multiple lines. This gave her the knowledge of competition, budgeting, order entry, floor merchandising, and markdown trends that is needed for these types of positions. This rep now holds the title of account executive for an accessory company.

SELLING PRODUCT LINES

Another great way to create experience, develop your selling skills, bring in extra income, and make an impact on your resume, is by selling a product line part-time. Russ, a college student, spent a summer selling a line of steak knives. He felt his time had been well spent. "I not only learned how to sell," he said, "but I gained necessary sales experience before graduation, while at the same time earning money."

A sales rep who now works for an industrial soap company selling soap products to institutional accounts such as hospitals, restaurants, hotels, and office buildings, gained experience by selling home party products on a part-time basis while she worked as a secretary. She did well and used this experience to land a better sales position. She now makes more than $45,000 a year, has use of a company car, and receives medical and other benefits. And she continues to sell her party product line.

Another rep started by selling Mary Kay products. She attended women's auxiliary rotary club benefits and Junior League meetings, and sold as much as $2,000 worth of makeup at one time. She is proof that if you are self-motivated and create your own experience, you can succeed at sales.

Selling knives or makeup and doing it well demonstrates your ability to sell virtually any product. There is an entire range of product possibilities in sales including several new multilevel selling positions in vitamins, phone service, makeup, party products, clothing, and more.

There are countless opportunities for selling product lines to gain experience. Try contacting one of the companies listed below, or look in your local library or on the Internet for additional companies.

Wachters' Organic Sea Products Corp.
360 Shaw Road
South San Francisco, CA 94080
(415) 588-9567
Nutritional/personal care/environmental products
Cost: $49

Natural World
7373 Scottsdale Road
Scottsdale, AZ 85253
(602) 905-1110
Personal care/home-cleaning products
Cost $39

Tiara Exclusives
717 East Street
Dunkirk, IN 47336
(317) 768-7821
Glassware
Cost: $60-75

Strawser Specialty Co.
1318-B South Finley Road
Lombard, IL 60148-4316
(708) 932-1635
Party-plan merchandising
Cost: $19

Brightideas
P.O. Box 1034
Concord, MA 01742
(508) 371-9040
Educational software for children
Cost: $395+

PART-TIME OR TEMPORARY SALES POSITIONS

Many companies are decreasing sales rep hiring and are instead hiring part-time service-rep positions. The key to obtaining an interview is to find out about these positions through contacts *before* they reach the newspaper. Managers can receive hundreds of responses from one newspaper ad. Therefore, if you are looking strategically, you may be fortunate enough to find out about the position before it is advertised. If you learn of an opening, arrange to have your resume hand delivered to the manager.

Sometimes companies create temporary sales position for as brief a period as six weeks to a few months. Recruiters are looking to place reps with such companies. One woman, who already worked in sales for an airline, wanted to go into pharmaceutical sales. She kept sending in her resume and finally landed a part-time position for a few weeks selling for an over-the-counter drug company, introducing a new product to the market. Since she worked odd hours at her airline job, she was able to handle the outside part-time sales position in the afternoon. The assignment lasted only a few weeks, but she had the opportunity of going to the stores, meeting other reps, and asking about available full-time positions while she gained sales experience in the industry of her choice.

"To be successful in business you've got to be like a quail dog. You know something is out there; you've just got to keep hunting and looking until you find it"

Anonymous

65

Developing Sales Skills: Professional Sales Training Courses

SEVERAL STEPS ARE ESSENTIAL TO THE process of finding a sales position. You must gain knowledge of the selling process, develop skills required for selling, and make contacts with other sales people. Attending sales courses and seminars is a perfect way to accomplish all of these steps at once—even if you have no prior experi-ence with sales. The courses and seminars recommended in this chapter are the courses that many Fortune 500 companies select to train their sales reps. They are some of the most highly regarded courses in the sales industry. Each sales seminar and training company represented here can provide you with a reference listing of their clientele. You will not only gain a better idea of the student profile for each seminar or training course from such a listing, but you may even find that a partic-

Good training can help overcome your shortcomings. When NFL running back Herschel Walker was in junior high school, he wanted to play football, but the coach told him he was too small. He advised Herschel to go out for track. Instead of taking the coach's advice, he under took a training program to build himself up. A few years later, he won the Heisman Trophy.

ular company you have targeted in your job search is listed as a client. What better way to gain experience and make valuable contacts?

How Sales Courses Can Help

Taking sales courses and seminars will provide an opportunity to:

- Gain familiarity with sales jargon.
- Demonstrate a "willingness to learn" image.
- Demonstrate that you are a self-starter and are serious about a career in sales.
- Project yourself as a professional.
- Build credentials—"sales experience and sales skills"—for your resume.
- Build needed knowledge of the basics of "how to sell."
- Create documentation for your Atta-Way File.
- Promote the image of a "a potential producer" instead of a "consumer of company funds."
- Provide an opportunity to make more contacts to further your job search.

The sales language you need to learn is unique to each specific sales industry, and the more contact you make with people in your chosen area the more you'll sound like them. In addition, the more familiar you become with the lingo, the more confidence you'll have when you interview.

> "Education is an investment—and never an expense."
>
> Nick Goble,
> Pennsylvania School
> Boards Association

Furthermore, creating experience and making contacts are the "dynamic duo" for gaining employment. Both are key elements to building the framework for your job search. When you start getting interviews through the contacts you've made, you'll want the confidence a few basic sales courses can instill. With a basic knowledge of the sales industry and the fundamentals of "how to sell " under your belt, you will be able to demonstrate on an interview that you can perform the necessary duties and responsibilities of a sales position.

Just as importantly, attending courses and seminars gets you in touch with other candidates, managers, and reps. As you attend courses and develop relationships, these contacts will become credible reference sources. Through them, you will find positions faster than job-seekers who lack such connections. Eventually, many of these contacts may even play supportive roles in your career. Once you start developing friendships within the sales circle, you will learn a great deal more about sales than your competition. If your goal is a job in sales, it

> "Money spent on the brain is never spent in vain."
>
> *Joe L. Griffith*

is imperative that you start making contacts as soon as possible. Start building this support system now by spending the money to attend one of the sales courses listed in this chapter.

CHOOSING A SALES COURSE

Below are listed seminars and continuing education classes that range from as little as $49 to as much as $3,000. The choice you make should be based on your budget, the time you have to take the courses, and your desire to be the most prepared sales applicant. As mentioned earlier, these courses are used by many Fortune 500 companies as well as smaller companies to train their sales forces. The course selections were based on a survey of more than 100 sales reps and managers that found these courses to be among the most respected and most frequently taken courses in the sales industry.

Much of this information was gathered by a recruiter from the resumes of successful sales managers and sales representatives she has helped over the years. Also included are career advice courses and skill-building courses offered by such companies as Career Track Seminars, Inc. and Skillpath Seminars, Inc.

To help you make direct contact with the organizations and companies producing these sales courses, names and phone numbers of the companies sponsoring the courses are also given, as are the prices. Be aware that these prices, phone numbers, and course offerings were accurate at the time of this writing but are subject to change.

After you read through the list, call each company to obtain literature packets and course outlines. They will also be able to provide information about specific fees, schedules of dates and locations, and estimates of additional costs such as lodging, meals, and transportation. Be sure to get details about the materials that accompany each course. Many include books, tapes, dayplanners, education credits, or certificates of completion with the price of the course. Most of the companies will either mail or fax the information. The more information you collect, the better prepared you will be to decide which course is best for your situation.

A word of caution: Some companies are much quicker than others to send the requested information. In fact, some companies may fail to send the information at all when first contacted. Keep a record of who you have called and check off each company as you receive the information. If you do not receive the information after two or three weeks, call the company back and re-request it. Sales seminar companies are swamped with requests, and yours may get overlooked.

Some of the courses offer participants a certificate good toward continuing education and college credit. If you are in undergraduate or graduate school, you should check with the business school office to determine whether these certificates would apply toward credits needed for a degree.

In addition to sales seminars and courses, many of these companies have catalogs. These companies sell a wide range of products, including books and tapes for developing sales skills, motivational skills, and many other skills necessary to perform well on the job. Always ask for a catalog of *all* of the products and courses they offer.

Sales Courses and Skill-Development Seminars

The Document Company Xerox
800-533-7287

Buyer-Focused Sales	*Skills Training*
4 1/2-day program	2-day program
$1,995	$995

Classes are held in Leesburg, Virginia, and tuition and room and board prices will be quoted. There is also a commuter rate. (A complete packet of information is available from the company). This is an excellent course for the new hire to the seasoned veteran.

Dale Carnegie Training
Corporate Headquarters
516-248-5100

Sales Advantage	*Dale Carnegie Course*
$1,095	$995

The training centers offer two courses for the entry-level candidate. In some states credit is given and continuing education credits are applicable. An advantage is that Dale Carnegie Training centers are located in most major cities.

The Zig Ziglar Corporation
800-527-0306

Sell by Design	*Effective Business Presentations*
$395	$695

Two day seminars are held in Carrollton, Texas. Gives CEU's to students. Managers often recommend reading Zig Ziglar's books and listening to the tape series.

Wilson Learning
Orlando, FL 800-255-0675
Eden Prairie, MN 612-944-2880

The Versatile Sales Person	*The Counselor Sales Person*
(2-day seminar)	(3-day seminar)
$750	$925

Classes are held in Orlando, Florida; Eden Prairie, Minnesota; and in regional offices. Call for information on locations and dates. Excellent sales courses for the beginner.

Robbins Research International, Inc.
800-535-6285

Unleash The Power Within Weekend	*The Competitive Edge*	*Date With Destiny*
3 1/2 days		1 day
$695	$199	$2,995

Tom Hopkins International
800-528-0446

Best of Tom Hopkins	*Boot Camp*
(6-hour seminar)	(2- to 3-day seminar held in 2-3 locations per year)
$159-$199	$595

You must call to obtain a list of locations and times.

Miller Heiman
800-526-6400

Strategic Selling	*Conceptual Selling*
$1,295	$1,295

Public sessions are two-day seminars; tuition includes light breakfast and lunch. Must be in sales part time, sub-repping, or have previous selling experience to participate in group sessions.

American Management Association

800-262-9699

Fundamental Selling Techniques for the New or Prospective	*Principles of Professional Selling*	*How to Develop and Maintain Positive Sales Relationships*
2 days	4 days	2 days
$1,375	$1,360	$1,370

The Fundamental Selling Techniques seminar is recommended for new salespeople with 0-6 months of sales experience. The Principles of Professional Selling is recommended for professionals with a minimum of six months experience.

Learning International

800-462-2545

Professional Selling Skills	*Winning Sales Conversations: Asking the Right Questions*
3 days	1 day
$1,395	$495

Recommended for both new and experienced salespeople.

Professional Training

800-247-9145, 801-225-5513
The Guerrilla Selling Seminar
1 day
$195

Solution Selling

Michael Bosworth
619-756-9730

Implementation Workshop	*Solution Selling Workshop*
3-day workshop	4-day workshop
$1,500	$1,600

Covey Leadership Center
(Motivational and Organizational Skills)
800-882-6839

The 7 Habits of Highly Effective People	*First Thing's First*
	Time Management
$1,495	$295

Public sessions offer one- and three-day intensive workshops, and include breakfast and lunch.

Franklin Quest
(Franklin Day Planner)
800-963-1776

| *Planning for Results* | *Presentation Advantage* | *Writing Advantage* |
| $159–$199 | $195 | $195 |

Teaches the skills and tools to plan, organize, and coordinate projects. Prices may vary if you purchase their planner.

Skillpath Seminars
800-873-7545

Holds one-day seminars and markets a wide variety of videos, audiocassettes, and books. Prices range from $59 to $395. They offer more than 30 seminar topics held across the country. Call for a catalog and a schedule of seminars and to get on their monthly mailing list.

Career Track Skill-Building Seminars
800-334-6780

Offers one-day seminars with a wide variety of topics. Prices range from $49 to $145. These seminars will help you learn a variety of skills, including oral and written communication skills, time management, and interpersonal skills, among others. In addition, Career Track sells a wide variety of tapes that apply to sales and developing sales skills. There is a catalog available and the company will send mailers on upcoming seminars scheduled in your city.

National Seminars Group
800-258-7246

Offers one-day seminars for career development, as well as tapes and books. Prices range from $69 to $395. Catalogs are available that list the seminars offered and schedules of dates and cities.

NAFE (National Association of Female Executives)
800-927-6233

NAFE, the largest organization of female executives, offers skill-building seminars, satellite conferences, and on-line products, including a resume service and resume database available to companies for recruitment purposes. The emphasis is on networking and career development for female executives. To join call for a membership form and information. Membership is $29 per year.

Toastmasters
800-993-7732

This is a club made up of 20 to 30 people who meet regularly (usually once a week) to develop, organize, and deliver oral presentations. Develop strong listening and evaluation skills. Toastmaster clubs are all over the world and have 8,000 clubs in 52 countries. To join, a $16 initiation fee provides you with a complete new member kit of educational materials. Annual international dues are only $36. Call to request schedules for meetings held in your area. On the Internet http:\ \www.toastmasters.org.

Chamber of Commerce
Many chambers offer a wide variety of networking meetings and invite speakers to General Membership Luncheons, Business After Hours, and Breakfast Round Table discussions. These meetings offer some skill-building seminars and provide an excellent opportunity to meet people. Many chambers have lists of the members by occupation. Some chambers sponsor trade shows once a year that may include exhibitors, seminars, and even placement agencies.

Many chambers provide "Job-Seekers Kits" and other resources from their Research and Information Departments. Call your local Chamber of Commerce for a schedule of events and for further information about joining. Readers in smaller communities may want to try a chamber in a nearby larger city. Most meetings can be attended for as little as $10, but membership dues will vary from city to city.

Community Colleges/Adult Continuing Education Classes
Community colleges offer sales courses and skill-building courses for minimal fees. Classes can range from "An Introduction to Selling" to "Presentation Skills." Often courses are taught by sales professionals or employees of seminar companies. The fees are lower, but the same information is taught. However, these types of classes may be harder to find. Try asking whether the instructor works for one of the seminar companies. Call around to several colleges and ask questions. Most classes cost somewhere between $49 and $149.

TAPES AND BOOKS

If you can't find the time or financial resources to enroll in a sales seminar, don't despair! Books and tapes on sales are certainly excellent alternatives. Listening to tapes can help you develop an ear for sales lingo as well as teach you the skills needed to sell. The benefit of listening to tapes is that you can do it just about anywhere—driving to work or school, cleaning your house or apartment, or even while jogging or working out. There are several ways to acquire these books or tapes with minimal financial investment. Many cities have books-on-tape rental stores, half-price book stores, and libraries. Tapes can be rented at books-on-tape rental stores for a minimal fee—anywhere from $4 and up. The library at a college or university may have a good selection from which to choose.

There is no excuse for any sales candidate not to read at least one or two sales books to develop sales skills and other necessary skills. Most of the companies listed above sell tapes and books in their catalogs along with their sales courses.

Listening to tapes and reading books should be a priority before you go on any interviews. The benefits of listening to tapes and reading books are similar to the benefits of attending seminars:

> "Read the best books first, or you may not have a chance to read them at all."
>
> *Henry David Thoreau*

- You will become familiar with the sales vocabulary.
- You will gain examples (that you can cite during interviews) of how you have taken the initiative to develop necessary selling skills.
- You will acquire the knowledge and skills necessary to perform the duties and responsibilities of a sales rep.

Although reading books and listening to tapes do provide many of the same benefits as attending seminars and sales courses, there are several disadvantages to using this method alone. First, if you, like many entry-level job candidates, lack sales experience, you will miss out on the opportunity to list a sales course on your resume under "Education and Seminars." Although you may learn just as much from a book as from a sales course, the sales course, unlike the book, can be listed on your resume. If you lack solid experience, this is just what you may need to catch a sales manager's attention.

Another drawback of not attending these programs is that you will not receive an attendance certificate for your Atta-Way File that states that you've had formal sales training. As we've already seen, an Atta-Way File can not only help your confidence level, but can also help impress a manager during an interview. A third drawback is that by not attending seminars you will miss wonderful opportunities to make contacts and connections with a variety of people in a business environment. The more opportunities you have to interact with other sales professionals and to hear them discuss their jobs and what they do to perform them, the more you'll learn. You'll also miss chances to meet sales reps and managers who may have information concerning job openings. You never know who may sit next to you in class; it may be a sales rep who is about to get promoted or whose colleague has recently vacated a position. Finally, if you try to gain sales skills solely by reading books, there will be no instructor to consult when you have questions.

Books and tapes may not provide the full advantages of sales seminars, but books and tapes are nevertheless important ways to expand your knowledge base and stay fresh for interviews.

Below is a list of suggested sales books and tapes. This list is far from complete and is only a suggested reading list. There are many choices of books available in book stores, libraries, or books-on-tape rental stores. The selected volumes will help you project yourself as having the knowledge and experience needed for the kind of position you're looking for. Anytime you make a contact, ask what books she has read that are beneficial in her specific industry. Some books may be geared more toward particular industries. Books that are excellent choices for consumer or medical sales people may not be so helpful if you are selling apparel or recreational equipment.

> "Thinking is easy, acting is difficult, and to put one's thoughts into action is the most difficult thing in the world."
>
> Johann Wolfgang von Goethe

BOOKS ON SELLING

- *Selling for Dummies.* Tom Hopkins. (IDG Books.)
- *Spin Selling.* Neil Racham. (McGraw-Hill, Inc.)
- *High Efficiency Selling.* Stephan Schiffman. (John Wiley & Sons, Inc.)

- *Guerrilla Selling.* Jay Conrad Levinson, Bill Gallagher, Ph.D., and Orval Ray Wilson. (Houghton Mifflin Company.)
- *Strategic Selling.* Robert B. Miller and Stephen E. Heiman. (Warner Books.)
- *Sales Shock.* Mack Hanan. (AMACOM.)

6

Selling Yourself:
Tips for Attention-Grabbing Resumes

SALES MANAGERS AND HUMAN RESOURCE DEPARTMENTS
have to scan through countless numbers of resumes. To keep your
resume out of their rejection pile, you must give them what they are
looking for. This chapter is designed to
give you tips on the easiest way to write
your resume to avoid scanning rejection.
Because there are already many books on
the topics of resumes and cover letters,
there is no reason to reinvent the wheel.
Any of these books can help you write a
basic resume. For this reason, I'll focus on
tips for writing resumes and cover letters specifically for sales reps.
You'll learn how to convey the impression that you have the
desired background and qualifications for a position even if you
don't already have sales experience. You will become more aware of
what your resume and cover letters must accomplish, as well as the
importance of letting others critique your resume and of using their
feedback to make revisions.

> "A resume is a balance
> sheet without any
> liabilities."
>
> *Robert Half, president,*
> *Robert Half*
> *International*

81

Think of your resume the way the publisher of a magazine would think about the cover of his magazines. Magazine covers are designed to grab the consumer's attention using catchy headlines and photos of good-looking men and women. Because the cover is the first thing you see—not the articles—its sole purpose is to catch attention and bring readers in for a closer look. Look at any GQ, Vogue, or Cosmopolitan. These magazines use key words on the cover such as "fashion updates," "designer looks," "staying in shape," "staying young," "sex," "love," and other arresting phrases to get you to buy the magazine. They know what you want to read, and they give it to you right up front—on the cover.

Make your resume and cover letter as arresting and irresistible as a magazine cover. You want a sales manager to take action by picking it up, glancing over the contents, and then phoning you for an interview. Your resume has to attract a sales manager the way a good magazine cover attracts consumers. A magazine publisher creates a need to read his magazine by understanding his readers' needs. Likewise, you have to create a resume that fits the needs of the sales manager and convinces him that you can fulfill those needs. By following the suggestions in this chapter, you will develop a resume that a sales manager will read and take seriously.

> "People don't read today; they flip."
>
> John Lyons,
> advertising and
> communications writer

Take Advantage of Resources

Because of the many resume books and other resources available in bookstores and libraries, writing your resume will be one of the easiest tasks of your job search. Nearly all resume guides provide numerous examples for career changers, graduating students, and students applying for internships. Software programs are available that make it even easier to write your own resume. Many people don't like to write resumes and swear by professional resume services, but with so many books available with examples to use as a guide, there's no reason not to create your own.

The following books are appropriate for the needs of someone searching for an entry-level sales job:

- *Trashproof Resumes*. Timothy D. Haft. (Random House, Inc.)
- *Designing the Perfect Resume*. Pat Criscito. (CPS, Barrons)
- *High Impact Resumes & Letters*. Ronald L. Krannich and William J. Banis, Ph.Ds. (Impact Publications.)

Although these three books provide good sample resumes and are a good place to start, this list is by no means exhaustive. Don't limit your resources. Do some browsing, and find a book that is right for *your* needs.

The first step most resume experts recommend is to fill out a personal information questionnaire as thoroughly as possible. Most resume books, including the ones listed above, provide such worksheets, asking questions in the following areas: Personal history, education and seminars, work experience, skills, activities, campus involvement, achievements, hobbies, and club memberships. Do not avoid this step. It is vital to accurately write as much information about yourself as you can put onto paper. List anything you feel would help convince a manager that you are the best candidate for a position. Managers don't look only for sales experience. They're also interested in accomplishments in other areas of your life, such as school, the military, sports, etc. Emphasize the following:

- High grade point average
- Honors classes
- Previous internship or part-time sales experience (i.e. retail, multilevel sales, or sub-repping)

- Involvement in campus activities (sororities, fraternities, or other organizations)
- Work experience while attending school
- Awards and honors
- Club involvement
- Military experience
- Competitive sports—high school, college, or professional
- Offices held or membership in social, community service, or other organizations
- Sales courses
- Work programs
- Volunteer work

Put down anything that puts you in a positive light. Be innovative. Include the time you received a top score on a marketing paper or came up with a creative idea for a product or project. Don't worry about dates—you can go back later and fill them in.

"And blow your own trumpet, or trust me, you haven't a chance."

William Schwenck Gilbet, English playwright

Resume writing does not have to be a chore. If you don't like doing this step by yourself, invite a friend, your mom or dad, spouse, professor, relative, coworker, or significant other over for pizza and have them ask you the questions and let them fill in the information. They may be able to remind you of an accomplishment, achievement, or award you've forgotten to mention. Your dinner guest will enjoy both the pizza and interviewing you. Involving a friend will help to coach you through the process of resume building as well as build interviewing skills. It will give you a chance to practice for the big day and start to learn how to verbalize your answers.

A resume is a glance at your past, a place to remember the positives and highlight those accomplishments for the reader. The questions provided in resume book worksheets are the same types of questions managers ask on interviews. "Tell me about your background. Let's start with college." This is the most common question you will have to answer on interviews, and it is almost always the opening question when it comes time to review the resume. If you avoid this step, your resume will not contain good information to review.

> "Everybody looks good on paper."
>
> *John Y. Brown, former governor of Kentucky*

Remember that you are the person who knows the most about what you do every day, what you have accomplished, and what skills you possess. You just have to use a little creative writing to make it look like you have the precise background and experience the interviewing sales manager has defined for a particular position. The key is to make it look and sound like the samples in the books. The following sentences were taken from the resumes of several sales reps working in a variety of industries. They are good examples of what sales managers are accustomed to seeing:

- Communicated with buyers, merchandise managers, department managers, and sales associates to obtain better floor space, mannequins in store windows, and special events.
- Organized monthly and seasonal calendars that followed set budget guidelines.
- Increased usage of promotional/educational materials such as merchandise books on the selling floor.
- Participated in New York market and Dallas regional market.
- Increased retail sales 62.8% from Fall 1990 to Fall 1991.
- Trained and supervised four interns.
- Ranked #1 in sales, consistently meeting or exceeding all monthly and yearly quotas, performing at 40% higher than all other sales representatives.
- Exceeded 100% of sales targets in first full year.

- Managed a highly competitive territory of 50 independent and chain accounts.
- Gained valuable sales skills and training by completing Intensive Sales Training Program.
- Re-established business relations with key accounts through improved service and fulfillment of customer needs.
- Established new business through cold callings, telemarketing, and mailings.
- Responsible for monthly budget selling a full line of copier and facsimile products.
- Started in an entry-level position and progressed to senior status with increased sales responsibilities.
- Organized and implemented city-wide education programs for existing and potential customers.
- Proven sales campaign winner through creative programming and effective presentations.
- Consistently exceeded company objectives by demonstrating proper surgical application of all products to surgeons, nurses, and other medical/surgical personnel.
- Demonstrated products representing technological advances in the mining and petrochemical industries.

If you don't have previous sales experience, internships, or part-time sales positions in your background, then you must write your job descriptions, achievements, and qualifications in the terminology that sales representatives use to describe their backgrounds. Managers are accustomed to seeing certain words, so choose your words wisely. Just remember, sales managers receive many resumes, so they scan them quickly. It isn't until the interview that they really get into discussing your background.

Lead off with your objectives, list your education next, followed by any seminars or training courses you have attended. List skills next, saving work history or experience for last. This way, by the time a sales manager gets to the work history, he will have seen the terminology an experienced sales professional would use. Your objective should have sales terminology in it; you will have attended sales seminars and skill-building seminars, and you will have developed sales skills. Ideally, these sections on your resume will give the impression that you have sold something along the way. Is this a little misleading? Who cares! It may be your best shot at an interview. Besides, it's the manager's job to scan. Your goal is simply to get in front of the sales manager.

> "All things being equal, the career person who is going to get ahead is not going to get ahead because he does great work. That is a given. We expect that. What will get him ahead is the edge he creates."
>
> *Jeffrey P. Davidson, marketing consultant*

CAREER CHANGERS

Over the years I have met many ex-teachers who became sales representatives. Many sales managers will hire teachers because of their presentation, organizational, verbal, and writing skills. In addition to teachers, I have met lawyers, engineers, and many other professionals who chose to leave their original fields. All have said it was difficult getting in and that creative resume writing was essential. For instance, a teacher might write her resume to resemble a sales rep's in the following way:

- Prepared and wrote multiple syllabi each semester using the latest textbooks for teaching Business English.
- Developed tutoring program for students, which accomplished an increase in GPAs.
- Utilized creative presentations and examples to motivate students to learn.

- Consistently reported highest GPAs in the school district for eleventh grade Business English classes.
- Introduced and sold the use of computers in class. Awarded grant money for computers.
- Communicated with administrators and school board members, advising them of changes needed in the classroom.
- Proven award winner for performance of students.

No matter what your current field, you must state the skills you now possess and explain how they are identical to sales skills. If you are a lawyer and you stand up in front of a jury, then you possess excellent verbal and presentation skills. If you have to write your closing arguments, then you have excellent writing and planning skills.

SEEK OTHERS TO CRITIQUE AND REVISE

If you lack creative writing talents, finish writing your draft and then hire an editor or writer. An editor can help correct grammatical mistakes, add polish, and make editing suggestions for helping your resume to resemble a sales professional's instead of a student's, lawyer's, engineer's, teacher's, nurse's, or whatever your current profession may be. When looking for an editor, check newspapers or magazines for advertisements placed by freelancers, call a publishing company (they hire editorial assistants who may do sidework), or look for an English teacher at a local college or high school who may be willing to take on an assignment. A good editor can do wonders with words. When you hire one, have him edit both your resume and your cover letters.

Communication skills are more than just talking well.

Once you decide on an editor, set up an appointment and explain what your goals are. Show him the sample resumes and cover letters in the books you've chosen and explain that you want your resume and letters to resemble the ones in the books. Also, make a copy of the job description in Chapter Eight and explain the duties and responsibilities of the sales rep. Then your editor can help take your experience and accomplishments and write them to make you look like someone who can perform the job.

> "People judge you by what you say and write. I don't know a successful man in business who is not a good letter writer."
>
> L.A. McQueen, General Tire & Rubber executive

After you have your resume edited and typeset on disk, contact a few people for advice and obtain feedback before making your final copies. Recruiters, sales managers, or sales reps in the industry in which you want to work are your best choices for this. Try to get your draft in the hands of someone you may want to interview with—not your number one company, maybe, but a company down the list a bit. Ask the person who critiques your resume whether he would call you for an interview based on your resume. If a sales manager cannot be consulted, try a seasoned sales rep. Ask whether he could get his sales manager to critique your resume. If so, give him a copy so he can mark it up and give it back to you. You want feedback. If the managers make good suggestions, take your resume back to your editor and make the adjustments.

After you've had more than one person review your resume and you have made any adjustments, take the disk to a copy or print service and have the final version printed on resume-grade paper. Ask around within your target industry what the accepted standards are for submitting your resume, and then follow the norm. You don't want to overdo things by submitting your resume on expensive-looking paper when managers expect candidates to simply fax or e-mail them. Still, never mail a resume on low-grade paper. If in doubt, go for a high-quality but modest-looking stock. Always buy extra paper and envelopes for cover letters and resume mailings.

Cover Letters

Think of looking for a job in sales like an actor looking for his first part in a movie. Since it will be your first acting role, you may not have the necessary experience, but if you make the right presentation and possess the right skills, you may land the part. Interviewing and acting are a lot alike, but even actors have to put together a resume and a portfolio. Think of your cover letter as an actor's portfolio. An actor wants audition time, so he needs a portfolio that grabs the director's attention. Similarly, your cover letter must promote you as someone who *must* be interviewed for the part of the sales rep.

Writing your cover letter is the next step in the job search process. Cover letters are just like resumes—they have to be written to grab the manager's attention and not get thrown into the rejection pile. Although there are many cover letter books on the market, the following two are recommended as a place to start:

- *The Perfect Cover Letter*. Richard H. Beatty. (John Wiley & Sons.)
- *200 Letters for Job Hunters*. William S. Frank. (Ten Speed Press.)

These two books have detailed instructions and guidelines for writing your cover letters. Also, they have many examples of actual letters. As with your resume, write a draft of your cover letter, and then if you are not good at polishing, let someone edit the letter. Writers or editors can make your letter stand out in the pile.

Try hard to fit your letter on only one page. Remember to state why you are the best-prepared candidate for the position. Again, even if you do not have actual sales experience, you must draw from your experience and explain how your current position is similar to a sales position. The worksheets that you filled out for the resume should also be used to construct your cover letter. As with your resume, use Chapter Eight as your guide to the skills, duties, and responsibilities of a sales rep. Then match your skills to the skills needed for the sales rep's position. Consider what you have learned in this book and then describe the steps you've taken to become an experienced job candidate in your letter. Emphasize attempts to gain experience, such as taking sales courses, multilevel selling, sub-repping, working as an intern, holding a part-time sales position, creating a self-styled internship, or riding in the field with a sales rep. These experiences demonstrate that you are a self-starter who has trained himself to become an attractive job candidate. Initiative, persistence, and resourcefulness are all qualities a manager looks for in addition to job experience. If they see you have taken the initiative to take sales courses and work as a sub rep, their curiosity may be aroused enough to call and find out more about you.

> "In proportion to the development of his individuality, each person becomes more important to himself, and is therefore capable of being more valuable to others."
>
> *John Stuart Mill*

PROFESSIONAL RESUME SERVICES

I strongly suggest that you *not* let someone else write your resume entirely, but that you only get someone with excellent writing abilities to edit your resume and cover letters. Resume services charge anywhere from $50 to as much as $200 or more. Unfortunately, many job-seekers hire a resume service to write their first resume. The problem is that you can get a service that writes *bad* resumes. One sales rep tells the following story:

> I paid someone to do my first resume, and it was horrible. The person who wrote the resume was not actually a bad writer, but he

did not know me. I didn't know what accomplishments I should list, and neither did he. The resume was dull and boring, and it didn't convey who I was. Nor was it what any sales manager or human resource person wanted. I had over two hundred rejection letters to prove the point.

The resume sent the message: "Here is another college graduate with no experience and very few achievements or accomplishments in school—just the standard stuff that everyone writes. Period!"

This candidate's story illustrates perfectly why you should write your resume yourself and not hire a service the first time. No one knows your experiences and qualifications better than you do. *You* decide what information goes into the resume, not someone else. That's not to say you can't get help. Don't forget that a good editor can polish what you write so that the final product really shines.

If you are determined to go to a resume service, find one who you know has written an exceptional resume for someone else. Most resume writers do not have the experience that sales managers, sales reps, and recruiters have with scanning resumes for promising candidates. Ask how many resumes a service has produced for sales job candidates. Find out, too, the number of interviews that have been landed with the service's cover letters. Also, ask job-seekers who have used the service whether sales managers they have interviewed with or recruiters they've worked with have made positive comments on their resumes.

Ask to look at samples the writer has produced and inquire what steps he takes to write a resume. If he does not tell you the steps or if the steps are not similar to the ones listed in this chapter, then write it yourself. Also, determine whether the writer performs a personal interview to find out everything he can about your background and how it would apply to a specific position. If he just hands out profile forms for you to fill in, you may want to consider another service.

A Case Study

Below is a sample resume that a resume service did for one job-seeker, a nurse who wanted to change careers and break into medical sales. After paying to have the resume done, she paid another small fortune to mail the resume to literally dozens of companies without landing a single interview. Undaunted, she concluded her resume was ineffective, and she determined to revise it and try again. Using sample resumes from other nurses who had made similar career changes, she corrected the deficiencies in her resume. She used more action verbs to describe what equipment she'd used as a critical care nurse. Since she wanted to break into medical sales and she did not have sales experience, she strengthened her resume by emphasizing her knowledge of different medical products and their applications. More importantly she attended a sales course, joined the National Association of Female Executives (NAFE), and added these to her resume. Shortly after she reworked her resume, she started getting calls for interviews.

Here's a copy of her initial resume that was prepared by a professional resume service:

MEGAN FALCONER

123 Main Street   Dallas, Texas 76543   (555) 123-4567

OBJECTIVE: A position in marketing or sales using my education and experience in the medical field.

SUMMARY OF QUALIFICATIONS:
- More than three years experience as a professional registered nurse.
- Excellent communicator with good human relations skills.
- Expertise at interacting with medical professionals at all levels.
- Adaptable and responsive to change.
- Computer literate with experience using Windows, custom hospital software, and Word Perfect.
- Experienced in sales and customer service.

EXPERIENCE:
1/94 to Present - Registered Nurse
American Nursing Services, Inc., Dallas, Texas
Provide professional nursing care within a hospital setting. Specialize in ICU and Critical Care nursing. Provide medication and treatments per doctor's orders. Handle charting using a CRT. Work as member of a team

6/93 to 2/95 - Registered Nurse
Irving Healthcare Systems, Irving, Texas
Provided nursing care within the coronary care unit of a major medical facility. Supervised ward of 12 beds as charge nurse. Supervised staff nurses, aides, and medical techs. Charted medications, procedures, assessments and shift incidents.

3/92 to 5/93 - Registered Nurse
Carolina Medical Center, Charlotte, North Carolina
Provided nursing care for a 36-bed coronary post surgical unit. Worked with senior nursing students as a tutor in the Preceptor program. Performed other nursing duties.

3/86 to 3/90 - Customer Service Representative
Mutual Savings and Loan, Charlotte, North Carolina
Worked as customer sales and service representative with lending and investment accounts. Handled some teller duties.

EDUCATION:
5/92 - Associate's Degree in Nursing
Charlotte-Mecklenburg Hospital Authority-School of Nursing, Charlotte, NC.

1980 - Fashion Merchandising Diploma
American Business and Fashion Institute, Charlotte, NC.

PERSONAL DATA:
Nonsmoker   Willing to Travel   Health: Excellent

References furnished upon request.

Here's a copy of her resume after she revised it herself:

MEGAN FALCONER

123 Main Street   Dallas, Texas 76543   (555) 123-4567

OBJECTIVE
A position in marketing or sales using my education and experience in the medical field

SUMMARY OF QUALIFICATIONS
- More than four years experience as a professional critical care nurse
- Excellent communicator with good human relations skills
- Expertise at interacting with medical professionals at all levels
- Experienced in sales and customer service
- Computer literate with experience using Windows, Word Perfect, and custom hospital software

PROFESSIONAL EXPERIENCE
Registered Nurse, Medical/Surgical and Cardiovascular Intensive Care
St. Paul Medical Center, Dallas, Texas
1996-Present

Responsible for coordinating and delivering all aspects of care for critically ill adult medical/surgical intensive care patients and their families. Assist with insertion and management of arterial lines, Swan-Ganz catheters, temporary pacemakers, and chest tubes. Manage patients on assisted ventilation. Initiate and titrate vasopressors, vasodilators, and antiarrythmic medications. Proficient in EKG interpretation. Attend inservices by sales representatives and clinicians regarding new products and medications. Provide feedback for evaluation of products.

Registered Nurse, Critical Care
American Nursing Services, Inc., Dallas, Texas
1994-Present

Provide quality healthcare within hospitals throughout Dallas-Fort Worth area. Areas include Surgical Intensive Care, Coronary Care, Telemetry, and Day Surgery. Utilize variety of monitors and medical equipment. Accurately assess and provide immediate interventions as needed. Report,

evaluate and document interventions. Initiate patient teaching pre-oper-
atively and post-operatively.

Registered Nurse, Coronary Care Unit
Irving Healthcare Systems, Irving, Texas
1993-1995

Implemented nursing care to patients with complicated myocardial infarction, angina, stent placement, angioplasty, and other related medical
problems. Managed patients requiring Intra-Aortic Balloon Pumps,
thrombolytic therapy, and mechanical ventilation. Prepared patients for
cardiac catheterization, angioplasty, and stent placement. Assumed charge
nurse duties supervising RNs, LPNs, and nurse assistants.

Registered Nurse, Post Coronary Progressive Surgical Unit
Carolinas Medical Center, Charlotte, North Carolina
1992-1993

Provided primary care for post coronary artery bypass graft patients,
patients with myocardial infarction, angina, post cardiac catheterization,
and angioplasty. Acted as preceptor to senior nursing students during 12-
week internship. Conducted inservices for staff on new advances and
technology in post CABG patients.

Customer Service Representative
Mutual Savings and Loan Association, Charlotte, North Carolina
1986-1990

Established new customer accounts, certificates of deposit, and large
investment accounts. Negotiated interest rates to satisfy customers and
maintain investments at the institution. Responsible for completing and
reviewing consumer loan applications for processing.

Charlotte Trade Mart,
Charlotte, North Carolina
1980-1991

Modeled and assisted in sales of clothing lines part time during market
weeks.

EDUCATION
Associate's Degree in Nursing
Charlotte-Mecklenburg Hospital Authority School of Nursing, Charlotte, North Carolina
1992

Diploma in Fashion Merchandising
American Business and Fashion Institute, Charlotte, North Carolina
1980

CONTINUING EDUCATION
Consultive Selling
1996

Critical Care Internship
1993

PROFESSIONAL AFFILATIONS
National Association of Female Executives

In a comparison of the two resumes, it is clear that the second gives better descriptions of Megan's activities as a nurse in the Critical Care Unit of the hospital. She uses action verbs to describe her duties, making them sound much more similar to those of a sales rep. Also, she attended a sales training course so she would have a sales background. After revising her resume, she sent it out to several medical recruiters. Also, she had one of the recruiters critique it, because the recruiter had also been a nurse, a clinical sales rep for a medical company, a sales rep, and then a sales manager. Within one week she started receiving calls from recruiters for interviews.

"When I interview a job applicant, I am first interested in how he presents himself. How does he look? How is he dressed? What does he say? How does he answer my questions?"

Franklin Murphy, chairman, Times-Mirror

97

She soon attracted medical companies looking for qualified clinical sales candidates to perform product training for doctors. She landed a clinical sales position within ninety days.

7

Securing an Interview:
It's Not What You Know . . .

REFERRALS ARE ONE OF THE MOST COMMON AVENUES to landing a sales job. While gathering research for this book, I asked every sales rep I met how he broke into sales and landed his first sales position. The most frequent response was that a referral from another rep within the company had secured the interview. Some respondents had actually been referred by another rep or manager for every sales job they'd ever had. Although the majority of these reps made stabs at finding their first positions through other sources, they finally got their breaks because someone referred them.

> "Few people are successful unless a lot of other people want them to be."
>
> *Charlie Bower*

One sales rep's story of how she landed her first position with Nike is short and simple: She got a recommendation from her sister. Her sister had interviewed with Nike and was offered a position, but because she did not feel the job suited her personality, she recommended her sister instead. The manager had a lot of respect for his first candidate—enough to even act on her recommendation to hire a family member. This story demonstrates that how you get the job is not important—and that *who* you know may get you the job as often as *what* you know.

Because referrals are so important, more than a third of this book describes how and when to meet contacts in sales by being where the action is. You should now have several solid, practical ideas of how to start making contacts, from where to find them to what to say when you meet them. Once you've made a substantial number of contacts, it's important to understand how the referral process works. Your contacts may have a variety of motivations for referring you for a position.

WHY CONTACTS GIVE REFERRALS

There are four common reasons an insider will refer you to a position. The first is the most important: If a referral is hired, companies pay their employees a referral fee ranging from a few hundred dollars to as much as $1,500-5,000. Some of these companies may not use headhunters or recruiters to hire sales reps because paying an employee a fee is less expensive. A recruiter might charge anywhere from $4,000-7,000 or more to place a sales candidate. For this reason, it's essential to find out which of the companies you're interested in pay their employees fees for referring.

> "Very few people get to the top without being taken under the wing of an older person somewhere along the way."
>
> *Jean Paul Lyet, former CEO, Sperry*

A second reason a sales rep may refer another person for a position is to project an image to the company that he is a team player. Often, sales reps want to demonstrate to upper management that they want to help the company. The more qualified sales people a company hires, the better the company will do financially.

Sales reps may also want to recommend candidates to fill positions that they themselves are vacating by going to work for another company. These reps really have two motives: First, it is in their best interest to leave the company on good terms. Making a lasting final impression by recommending a good candidate to replace them is a great way to keep that good job reference intact. Secondly, they want to leave their customers in the hands of someone they trust. Reps work hard to build solid, friendly relationships with their managers, co-workers, and customers. Just because they leave a company for financial or purely private reasons, doesn't mean they don't still care about the company that gave them their first break. In these cases reps are apt to recommend a replacement they believe in.

Finally, a sales rep you're friendly with may inform you of a forthcoming opening *before* a newspaper ad runs. Finding a position this way is not as easy as with a personal referral, but if a rep tips you off on a job opening in his company, he may also be willing to let you use his name in a cover letter stating that he referred you to the position.

PROJECT YOURSELF AS A
REFERRAL-WORTHY CANDIDATE

In order to get referred, you need to think of employee referrals from the rep's or manager's perspective. Reps tend to refer people who fit a certain image they want to represent their company. They may look for candidates who:

- Project the right image,
- Will interview well by clearly and convincingly communicating their qualifications,

- Are ambitious and project enthusiasm,
- Have a positive attitude and an eagerness to learn more.

But how will projecting the right image or possessing these traits land you a referral? The following story is a good example of the intricate process of landing a sales rep position.

Jessica, a nurse who had lost her job at a local hospital, was interested in changing careers. She had no sales background, but she was determined to use her exceptional clinical background to find a position in pharmaceutical sales. She started the usual search by calling recruiters and answering ads in the newspaper. She had a friend in medical sales who knew she wanted to break into the field and who was willing to help. One day, her friend was at a local hospital when she decided to use the phone in the pharmacy. When she walked in, she noticed a pharmaceutical sales rep talking to the pharmacist. She recognized him as a sales rep because he had his detail bag with his supplies inside lying open on the floor next to counter. She made her phone calls, and then, as she was about to leave, she exchanged hellos with the rep. Jessica's friend asked what kind of work he did, then mentioned that she had a friend seeking a sales position. Since she herself had been so impressed with Jessica's enthusiasm and professionalism, she told the pharmaceutical rep about Jessica, painting a flattering picture of her qualifications and describing how she would be an asset to his company. He told her his company had an opening and gave her his business card with his direct supervisor's home number on it. See the importance of developing close relationships with people in a position to help you?

> Career advancement is much like marketing; your objective is to position yourself as the ideal solution to an organizational need.
>
> J. Paul Costello, president, Costello, Erdlen, & Company

USE CREATIVE QUESTIONING

When Jessica received the valuable new contact's phone number, she realized she had two important tasks ahead of her. First, she had to contact the sales rep to get as much information about the position, the manager, and the company as possible. She didn't want to talk to this rep as she would with just any new contact, because *this* contact was her direct connection to an actual job opening. She did not want to ask the broad questions she had asked of earlier contacts when she was collecting as much general information as possible. Rather, she wanted to use creative questioning to focus her inquiry toward one goal: Landing that open position. She needed to convey the professionalism, knowledge, and confidence of an experienced, well-qualified candidate. That way, she would not only gain valuable information from the contact, but she might also achieve her second task: Getting a referral.

At the very least, she knew the rep could give her insight into the job duties and responsibilities of this particular position, as well as information about the manager's personality, the things he looked for in a rep, his interviewing style, and more. With these aims in mind, she began formulating questions to ask the rep. Her goal was not only to get information, but also to reveal her qualifications, her knowledge, and her professionalism in the process. In short, to obtain the referral, she knew she must project the polished image he was looking for. To accomplish this, she did not ask simple straightforward questions, but instead phrased them in a way that would reveal something about herself. For example, instead of asking, "What kind of products would I be selling in this position?" she asked, "As a nurse, I've become highly familiar with the different manufacturers of drugs, as well as individual drugs' actions, indications and contraindications, dosages, and administrations. What particular kinds of pharmaceutical products would I be working with in this sales position?" By phrasing her question like this, Jessica was able to get the same information from the rep while at the same time demonstrating her knowledge of the kinds of products she would be working with.

Instead of asking, "What level of experience is the manager looking for in candidates for this position?" She asked, "As a nurse, I've worked closely with the reps who called on our hospital. I've observed the way they presented their information, and I've learned how important it is to be able to converse with doctors, administrators, and other personnel. Would experience interacting with hospital staff and communicating information I've learned at product in-services be an asset if I obtained this sales position?" This question not only got Jessica the rep's input on the kind of experience his manager was looking for, but also helped convince the rep that her background in nursing would help her perform the job even though she had no actual sales experience. By illustrating her qualifications to the rep through creative questioning, Jessica was able to project exactly the kind of image that would make the rep comfortable referring her for the position. At the end of the conversation, she simply asked the rep her final and most important question: Could she tell the manager that he had referred her for the position? Without hesitation, he agreed.

BE PREPARED FOR SETBACKS

Once she had obtained the sales rep's referral, Jessica phoned the sales manager and introduced herself. Her timing was perfect, because he was going through resumes and setting up interviews. But, this was when she hit Setback #1. She had not realized that the manager had run a blind ad in the classified section of the newspaper the week before and that she had already sent a resume to him. As she was introducing herself, he stopped her and said that he recognized her name from a resume, and that as a matter of fact, he'd just thrown it in the garbage can because she lacked sales experience.

At this point she could have politely thanked him and let it go at that, but she had learned too much in the course of her job search about the value of persistence. Instead she responded by telling him to pull her resume out of the garbage and give it a second look. She told the manager that she had his sales rep's recommendation and explained that the sales rep thought she might be the best candidate for the position. Next, she explained that she had something to offer that even an experienced sales rep did not have—a clinical background that would allow her to communicate with the physicians and nurses. At the end of their conversation the resume was out of the garbage, and she had an interview scheduled within two days.

Within a short time she had interviewed twice, and she was told she was the number one candidate. Shortly thereafter, she was promised an offer letter. Then came Setback #2. When no offer came within a few days, she got some very discouraging news: A hiring freeze had been instituted. The position was put on hold.

When a month had passed and the freeze continued, she accepted a position in another field and moved to another city. Before she moved, however, she asked the manager to keep her in the active file for positions and told him that she would stay in contact. She sent him a note with her new address and phone number as well as two more notes over the next six months. A few months later, he phoned her and told her he was recommending her for a sales position in her new city. She interviewed with the new manager and was soon hired.

> "People are always blaming their circumstances for what they are. I don't believe in circumstances. The people who get on in this world are the people who get up and look for the circumstances they want, and if they can't find them, make them.
>
> *George Bernard Shaw*

Ambitious people don't make excuses.

Even though Jessica didn't land the original position she sought, the referral process was still responsible for her eventual employ-ment. It started with one contact describing her to a rep as a profes-sional, qualified candidate. She re-enforced this image of herself by using creative questioning when she phoned the sales rep herself. As a result, he was more than willing to let her use his name when contacting the manager. She used her medical background and training to sell the manager on her technical skills rather than on her sales skills. She kept her relationship with the manager alive by persisting in her mail campaign. In the end, because of her first referral from the manager's rep, she landed a sales position with a pharmaceutical company in an entirely different city a year later. The steps she took to break into sales were actually very limited, but by developing a relationship with the sales rep and sales man-ager and by staying in contact with them, she was recommended for and received a sales rep position.

PERSISTENCE PAYS

Persistence is an essential quality for a potential sales candidate to have. No manager can be sure that he's hired the right person for a position. The number one candidate won't always make it. There are countless stories of sales reps being hired and then bombing out in sales training or in the first weeks or months in the territory. Likewise, sales candidates will occasionally accept a position with other intentions in mind, such as biding their time until a position comes open with another company. As unfair as that seems, it happens every day. One company interviewed and hired a rep, who was flown to the home office for sales training.

> "Nothing in the world can take the place of persistence."
>
> Calvin Coolidge

After the second day of class, he never showed up for training. What happened? He had received an offer for the position he had really wanted. He'd been the runner-up for that position, and the first-choice rep had bombed out in training, giving him the shot he needed. The rep's defection opened up the position at the first company, giving *that* runner-up a shot. You may have gone on several interviews and been ranked as the number two candidate. Even though you may not have been chosen the first go around, you may, like Jessica and these reps, get a second chance. At such times, it's nice to have an insider pulling for you.

Thus, when interviewing, if you really like a company, the manager, and the product, always follow up with a letter to the sales manager even if you do not get an offer the first time around. A few weeks later, send a fax or voice mail stating that you were disappointed you did not get the position, because you were especially excited about the company and the product. Even if someone else is hired or the position is put on hold, keep up a steady mail campaign. Let the interviewing sales manager know that you are still interested in the position, and that if the sales rep he hires does not work out, you would like to be considered. Send him Christmas cards or notes on a special occasion to keep yourself fresh in his memory.

> "There's no grander sight in the world than that of a person fired up with a great purpose, dominated by one unwavering aim."
>
> Orison Swett Marden

Showing interest is important, but take care to be tactful and not overly aggressive with your follow-up. A letter or two and maybe a voice mail will suffice. With follow-up and a little enthusiasm, one manager may refer you to another manager in the company—or in another company altogether. He may even tell a recruiter about you and suggest she try placing you because you are a great candidate. The point is to always maintain a professional image and to build relationships with sales managers and reps.

8

Knowing How to Answer: Finding Out What Interviewing Managers Expect

IN ORDER TO UNDERSTAND WHAT MANAGERS EXPECT from interviewees for entry-level sales positions, it is important to know the duties and responsibilities of both sales reps and sales managers as defined by upper management. Understanding the job responsibilities of the sales manager as well as those of the sales representative will give you a leg up over other less informed interviewees.

A general overview of both a manager's and a sales rep's job description is presented below. Most candidates applying for sales positions are not privy to this information unless they have friends or acquaintances in sales who could explain what they do every day as sales reps. In many cases job-seekers do not understand the importance of learning the specific responsibilities of both a sales representative and a sales manager. Many companies fail to write guidelines for the entry-level sales rep to follow, producing poor performers.

Ask any experienced sales professional under thirty-five years old

> "I believe the true road to preeminent success in any line is to make yourself master in that line.
>
> *Andrew Carnegie*

if he knew what he was doing on his first interview for a sales position. He will probably tell you no. In fact, many reps recalling their first interview make comments like, "I never knew what a rep did until I actually had the position," "I didn't have a clue what a rep did, I just made stuff up," or, "I went on the interview hoping I was what they were looking for." This is what most candidates do and why so many of them fail. Managers have to sift through the ones who obviously *don't* know to find the ones who *seem* to know what the job entails. After reading this chapter you will know more than ninety-nine percent of the candidates you will compete with on any interview for a position, giving you the competitive edge you need to get hired.

CORPORATE STRUCTURE OVERVIEW

Almost any company you interview with will be divided and subdivided into many groups and teams with specific responsibilities, and each of these groups will be headed by a person who is responsible for overseeing the work of those below him and who reports directly to someone above him. This structure holds true for everyone in the company—from the president or CEO in charge of the entire corporation down to the lowest manager who may supervise only a few employees. The structure of divisions and subdivisions that make up a company, of course, encompasses much more than simply sales managers and sales representatives. To fully understand where you, as a potential sales rep, stand in relation to the manager responsible for hiring you, you must first understand how this relationship fits into the larger structure of the corporation.

> "The single most important factor in determining the climate of an organization is the top executive."
>
> *Charles Galloway*

The next two diagrams represent organizational flow charts of a model company.

Sales

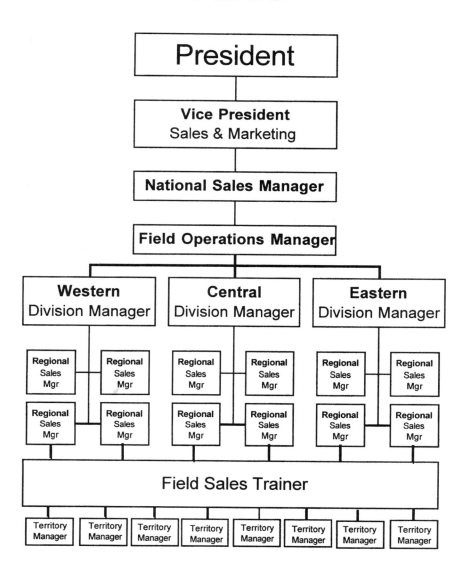

Marketing

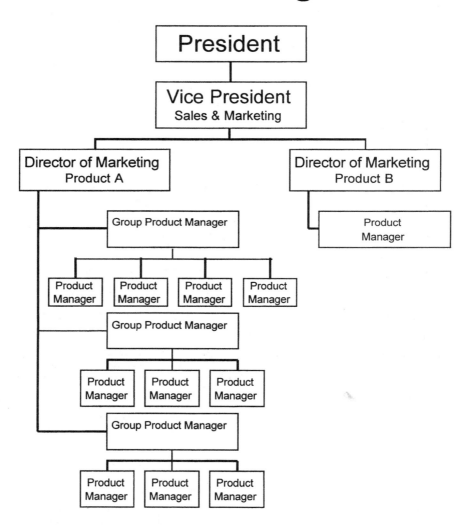

Though structures may vary from company to company, if you want to be a sales representative you need to become familiar with the squares and connecting lines of an organizational chart. Anybody who makes a presentation to new hires seems compelled to pull this chart out as an icebreaker at training and sales meetings. Start understanding these charts, whether you want to or not. Upper management wants you to learn the organizational chart so you will understand the chain of command.

Look at the bottom of the chart—picture the boxes there as the feet of a giant corporation. They function to support the entire body of this company. The fact is the sales reps (or the potential sales reps) will have to put on these boots and carry the weight. Sales reps are responsible for selling the products or the services of the company. They have the burden of making the sales numbers required to make a profit. When sales quotas are met, the weight of the company lightens. But when the numbers (sales quotas) are not met, the boots become harder to walk in as the weight they bear increases.

> A coach once said, "The players win, not the coach. The best thing a coach can do is get the best players in action and let them do their thing. The coach can lose for you, but he can't win for you." Managers, like coaches, are judged by the results of the people on their team.
>
> *Anonymous*

UNDERSTANDING THE MANAGER'S PERSPECTIVE

Understanding the manager's duties and responsibilities will be an asset to the sales candidate trying to get an interview. By becoming aware of the manager's job description, you can anticipate his needs and project the image that you can fulfill those needs. Also, you may be able to use knowledge of a manager's job description to discuss how you would effectively run a territory. Most sales job candidates haven't had an opportunity to read what a manager's duties and responsibilities entail. Whether you are developing a message for the manager's voice mail requesting an interview or writing and eye-catching cover letter, using the information listed will increase your chances of catching a manager's attention.

Managers can certainly assess whether a candidate has the knowledge and understanding of the sales position he is interviewing for, but they are far more impressed when a candidate understands a sales manager's responsibilities as well. Most interviewees spend their time talking about the duties of the sales position. But having the ability to discuss the position on a different level is likely to earn the candidate a higher rating. It demonstrates the candidate's assertiveness and his willingness to do what it takes to make the manager successful. In this respect, it also demonstrates teamwork and cooperation.

Finally, having the ability to converse in the same language and terminology used in the sales industry is a leg up on other entry-level candidates. Words like "establishing quotas," "setting budgets for the territory," and "tracking sales performance" are used every day by sales managers. Demonstrating such knowledge in an interview gives you a competitive edge.

Sales managers hold varying titles and oversee anywhere from one to ten or more sales people within each organization, depending on whether they are divisional or regional managers, and on the industry, the company's size, and its management structure.

During the job search process, sales candidates will quickly identify how the managers' titles are defined within the industry they have targeted for employment. In one fashion apparel company the managers are called, "Regional Managers," while in the medical or pharmaceutical industry they may be called "Divisional" or "National" Managers.

Whatever the industry, the sales manager's job performance (and the sales rep's job performance) is evaluated once a year for raises and promotions. A key aspect of the evaluation is, of course, the total number of sales generated by the manager and the reps under him. In short, the manager is evaluated not only on his personal accomplishments, but also on the accomplishments of everyone in his division. As a result, they are constantly asking themselves:

> "A good supervisor is a catalyst not a drill sergeant. He creates an atmosphere where intelligent people are willing to follow him. He doesn't command; he convinces."
>
> *Whitley J. David*

- How well is my sales team performing?
- Is my sales team making its sales numbers?
- Where does my division rank in the company as a whole?
- Is my division making a profit?

Therefore, a manager hires a sales professional based on her belief that the candidate can accomplish the task of reaching her sales goals set by upper management for her division or region.

A SALES MANAGERS JOB DESCRIPTION

- **Set** sales objectives and develop plans to achieve these goals for each territory.
- **Forecast** sales for upcoming year by examining sales reps' reports and sales projections for new, existing, and lost accounts.
- **Establish** quotas by using company's goals and objectives for division.
- **Set** budgets for each territory.

- **Create** strategies for team to cover sales territories efficiently and effectively.
- **Monitor** reps' sales and progress reports.
- **Recruit** and train sales reps.
- **Hire** and **fire** sales reps.
- **Track** performance of sales reps by analyzing sales rankings, sales reports, and contracts of new and existing accounts.
- **Motivate** sales representatives.
- **Work** with sales reps in their territories.
- **Accompany** reps on sales calls to assist in closing sales or making important presentations.
- **Strategize** with sales representatives to reach sales goals.
- **Negotiate** pricing for accounts and implement contracts.
- **Increase** profits and sales.
- **Decrease** turnover.
- **Develop** individual strengths of sales reps.
- **Attend** management meetings.
- **Participate** in conference calls.
- **Teach** sales classes.
- **Make** presentations at National Sales Meetings.
- **Mentor** sales reps.
- **Perform** yearly evaluations of sales reps' performance.

Understanding the duties and responsibilities of the manager gives the insight needed for a rep to work well with a sales manager. The reps know that the manager is there to help them in closing accounts and making important decisions, not just to criticize and monitor. By functioning as a team, the manager and the rep help the company reach its goals, thereby making them both more successful. Empathy is essential. Putting yourself in your manager's shoes and understanding what he's trying to get you to accomplish is half the battle.

How Managers Assess Performance

The manager is responsible for the sales numbers of all members of the sales force that report to him. That's pressure. He is held accountable and must strategize with his sales team on how to increase sales and reach the goals of the company. If all the reps are reaching their quotas he looks good to upper management. If even one is not making his quotas, an explanation is required. What tools do the managers have to help them analyze the individual rep's performance?

> "The function of a supervisor is to analyze results, not try to control how the job is done."
>
> Gary Jenkin, management consultant

The following reports show the hypothetical rankings of the individual sales reps, by product or service, region, and division. Once on board and in the territory, reps are mailed or faxed monthly sales figures, quarterly sales figures, and yearly sales figures. Each month a report will show a rep's current sales figures compared to the previous year's sales figures. Also, reports compare sales quotas to actual sales dollars to see whether those figures are being met. Most companies rank their reps from first place to last. The worst place in the world for a sales rep to be is last place on that list. Reps and managers live and breathe (and hire and fire) by the sales rankings.

Many sales managers break down the numbers into more defined reports. Frequently, sales managers develop newsletters or monthly reports on each rep's progress in his division. The newsletters contain grids and graphs that rank each rep's productivity and contribution to the division. This monthly mailer motivates the rep with the lowest rankings in the division to compete with his fellow reps. The worst thing for a rep—especially if he is competitive—is to see his territory at the bottom of the rankings. Can you already feel the pressure of what it takes to be a sales representative? Imagine how the manager feels while interviewing potential reps. He is trying to find a person with a highly developed competitive spirit: Someone who can take pressure, juggle all the balls, and develop the skills necessary to succeed.

Understanding the duties of sales managers makes it easy to see why they must be careful and selective when hiring a sales representative. If they hire the wrong person to fill a vacant territory, it can cost the company lots of money—which can have severe implications for a manager's job security.

Turnover is costly to the employer. Tom Gerrity, a founder of Index Systems, said that it cost his company about $20,000 to replace one employee. Turnover alone was taking $500,000 from the bottom line.

SALES REP RANKING
Product A

Territory	Name of Sales Rep	December Increase	December Rank	YTD $$Increase	YTD Rank
705	WASHINGTON	$20,546	3	$364,454	1
406	ADAMS	$23,334	2	$237,511	2
603	LINCOLN	$18,455	4	$188,922	3
703	EISENHOWER	$28,409	1	$178,438	4
406	NIXON	$12,087	7	$159,353	5
702	KENNEDY	$2,797	27	$155,783	6
405	FORD	$9,932	10	$152,109	7
707	CARTER	$12,567	6	$146,797	8
308	ROOSEVELT	$16,740	5	$145,996	9
905	REAGAN	$5,351	20	$127,371	10
301	HAMILTON	$8,464	13	$125,475	11
408	JEFFERSON	$5,477	19	$116,319	12

DIVISIONAL RANKING BY PRODUCT GROUP

Product Group	Division	December Increase	December Increase Per Sales Rep	December Rank	YTD Increase	YTD Increase Per Sales Rep	YTD Rank
A	NORTHEAST	$61,804.00	$8,829.00	1	$627,305.00	$89,615.00	1
A	GREATLAKES	$29,235.00	$3,654.00	2	$322,550.00	$40,319.00	2
A	WESTERN	$(4,838.00)	$(806.00)	3	$111,111.00	$18,519.00	3
A	MID-WEST	$(45,495.00)	$(7,583.00)	6	$32,681.00	$5,447.00	4
A	SOUTHEAST	$(64,719.00)	$(8,090.00)	7	$(40,762.00)	$(5,096.00)	5
A	MID-ATLANTIC	$(42,805.00)	$(7,134.00)	4	$(71,714.00)	$(11,952.00)	6
A	SOUTHWEST	$(58,051.00)	$(8,293.00)	8	$(150,395.00)	$(21,485.00)	7
A	NORTHWEST	$(43,465.00)	$(7,244.00)	5	$(131,296.00)	$(21,883.00)	8
B	GREAT LAKES	$18,172.00	$2,596.00	2	$311,953.00	$44,565.00	1
B	MID-ATLANTIC	$22,018.00	$3,145.00	1	$159,586.00	$22,798.00	2
B	MID-WEST	$(1,617.00)	$(202.00)	5	$170,247.00	$21,281.00	3
B	NORTHEAST	$(4,650.00)	$(775.00)	8	$114,796.00	$19,123.00	4
B	NORTHWEST		$2,262.00	3	$114,309.00	$19,052.00	5
B	SOUTHEAST	$(3,187.00)	$(531.00)	6	$104,886.00	$17,481.00	6
B	SOUTHWEST	$3,920.00	$490.00	4	$101,889.00	$12,736.00	7
B	WESTERN	$(3,512.00)	$(585.00)	7	$14,497.00	$2,416.00	8

DECEMBER INCREASE

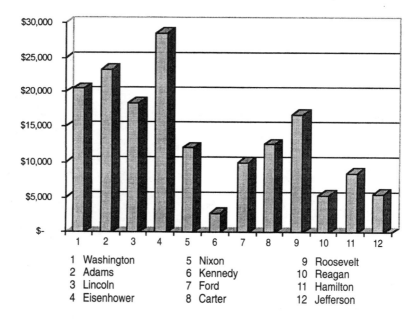

1 Washington	5 Nixon
2 Adams	6 Kennedy
3 Lincoln	7 Ford
4 Eisenhower	8 Carter

9 Roosevelt
10 Reagan
11 Hamilton
12 Jefferson

UNDERSTANDING THE DUTIES OF A SALES REP

Before a potential sales rep goes on an interview for either a sales position or a sales internship, he should request a copy of the job description. Knowing the specific goals and objectives of a company's management team will prepare you to position yourself as the person most able to help the interviewing sales manager reach his goals.

> "Nobody should think they can just coast though life on the basis of gifts that they have nothing to do with in the first place. You have to pay your dues and do your homework."
>
> *Steve Allen*

Sales managers hire sales representatives who either have the ability to perform these duties, or who have the aptitude to learn them. Below is a generic sales representative's job description. Although it is extensive, it is not meant to discourage you, but rather to give you a realistic picture of the scope of a sales rep's duties. Take note in this example of the action verbs used in each statement to describe the sales duties. Make these yours to be used in every interview.

A Sales Representative's Job Description

- **Support** and represent the corporate mission. Example: Deliver quality services and products to the customer; provide clients with cost-effective products and services; maintain an environment for employees that promotes self-actualization, professionalism, and security; optimize the return on stockholders' investments.
- **Attend** sales training, seminars, and conferences.
- **Learn** the full range of products and services offered.
- **Attend** national and divisional sales meetings.
- **Define** and identify opportunities for new sales.
- **Obtain** new accounts in assigned territory.
- **Create** and implement short- and long-range marketing/sales plans to ensure the profitability and growth of the territory.
- **Analyze** new opportunities to increase sales in existing accounts.
- **Establish** and build new business relationships with targeted accounts.
- **Perform** all necessary sales and marketing activities. Example: presentations, proposal writing, account development, strategic planning, preparation of account activity reports, organization of weekly and monthly calendars, and attending major trade shows, meetings, conventions, or markets.
- **Develop** and provide informative, periodic, written and verbal reports on activities and accomplishments performed in the territory to enhance management's understanding of business environment.

- **Achieve** satisfactory profit/loss ratio and share of sales performance in relation to preset budgeted standards and territory marketing/sales plan.
- **Collect, develop,** and **maintain** customer data and share with home office. Example: Account profiles on either computer database or hard copy.
- **Coordinate** account/sales efforts with divisional/regional manager and others to ensure effectiveness of all advertising, promotion, marketing, and sales tools.
- **Provide** input to company on competitive activity, pricing, and promotions.
- **Work** as a team member and communicate effectively with managers and home office personnel.
- **Evaluate** and give feedback concerning market reactions to advertising programs, packaging, etc., to ensure timely adjustment of marketing strategy and plans to meet changing market and competitive conditions.
- **Schedule** appointments with potential customers to make presentations.
- **Follow up** on leads from home office for territory.

Hire people with good judgment and you get good judgment. "You want people who can be honest with themselves in analyzing a situation, making judgments, and evaluating projects."
Donald Siebert, chairman, J.C. Penney

Although not exhaustive, this list is detailed enough to give you a good overview of a sales rep's job description. You should be able to apply this knowledge to all aspects of your job search. Understanding the job description allows you to think about situations that would occur on the job and in the interview. This knowledge will allow you to respond more appropriately in an interview because you will have more time before the interview to think how to answer questions in ways

that relate to the job description. To interview successfully and land a position is a
culmination of understanding the sales
process as much as it is about understanding the interviewing process. Having
this information allows you to go into the
interview more confident and certain of
yourself and your ability to relate to the
sales manager. An interview is just like a
test in school. If you have time to study for
a test and thoroughly understand the
material, then you will score much higher.

> "A wealth of skills
> doesn't ensure freedom
> any more than any other
> wealth, but it surely can
> expand choice, which
> may lead out of some
> corners."
>
> *Steward Brand,*
> *publisher*

Using Your Knowledge at the Interview

Now that you understand both the manager's and the sales rep's job
descriptions, you are ready to use your knowledge to prepare for the
interview. Having this knowledge will allow you to develop examples of skills that you currently possess that will translate into ones
needed for sales. If you take each of the rep's duties and develop a
statement describing ways in which you have performed tasks
requiring similar skills, you'll be able to demonstrate that you are
qualified to do the job.

The more skills we have, the more opportunities we have.

Using the company's job description as a guide the interviewer
begins the search for a sales candidate who possesses a preponder-
ance of the required skills. Often the interviewer asks the sales candidate to describe himself or describe how others view him. The
interviewer is not looking for a soul-searching self-analysis. He is
looking for clues that demonstrate that you possess certain skills
and qualities. The following is a list of skills and qualities that a
manager looks for in a job candidate. All of these qualities can be

developed through sales experience, but they can also be obtained from experience in other kinds of jobs or in school.

- Verbal presentation and written communication skills
- Telephone sales skills
- Time and territory management
- Empathy skills
- Organizational skills
- Problem-solving skills
- Entrepreneurial skills
- Strategic-planning skills
- Numbers-oriented mindset
- Success-oriented mindset
- Results-oriented mindset
- Competitive
- Problem solver
- Self-starter
- Ability to work independently, with little supervision or direction
- Ability to learn features and benefits of the products and services offered by the company and its competitors
- Polish
- Professional image
- Proper business etiquette
- Articulate
- Self-motivation
- Goal-oriented
- Team player
- Sales-related experience
- Integrity
- Trustworthiness

In addition to the above list, managers look for people who are willing to make a commitment to the company if hired. Sales representatives are required to work from home or home offices' headquarters and travel to meet with clients, potential clients, and others to acquire and develop potential business. They must have the ability to work a minimum of forty hours per week, and often more. In addition, reps are required to attend meetings and tradeshows, which are typically on weekends and even holidays. In short, you must be able to convey in the interview not only that you possess the above skills, but that you are committed enough to put them to work.

> "I have found enthusiasm for work to be the most priceless ingredient in any recipe for success."
>
> *Samuel Goldwyn*

You will need to develop examples of how you fit this profile. Look for instance, at the first skill listed: Verbal presentation and written communications. Figure out concrete examples that demonstrate that you possess this skill. Maybe you are a lawyer in the midst of a career change. A lawyer presents his client's position to the judge or jury. Maybe you are a student who took a speech or presentation skills class and made an A in the class. Maybe you minored in English or majored in English or journalism. Always be prepared to give examples of how you have developed these requisite skills.

Perhaps focus on four or five of these skills and come up with a list of concrete ways to demonstrate you possess them. The interviewer is less interested in the candidate saying that they posses good communication skills as he is in hearing you talk about concrete instances in which you demonstrated these skills and got good results. In other words, show him that you possess these skills by offering examples—don't just tell him.

For instance, one job candidate wanted to convince her interviewer that she was a self-starter with good organizational skills. She was a nurse who was seeking a job change. In her job, she often went the extra mile by keeping notes and handouts that medical sales reps left when they performed training on the products and drugs she used in the Intensive Care Unit. At the conclusion of each in-service, she asked each rep for a packet of literature and package inserts for the products they trained on. She did this so that she could refer back to her notes and the literature in case anyone forgot how the product worked. By keeping these files, she demonstrated good organizational skills and that she had the ability to learn the features and benefits of products from the numerous companies whose drugs and equipment she worked with.

Not many of her colleagues did what she did, but when they needed information on a drug or product, they would ask her if she had her handouts. She demonstrated several other skills by using this example. It demonstrated that she possessed problem-solving skills by keeping good reference materials, that she was self-motivated, and that she was a team player by sharing her files. So in her sales job interview, she used to her advantage what at first seemed like unrelated experience by demonstrating that her organizational skills helped her become a resource person for the other nurses on the unit. Also, working independently is one major skill a nurse needs because she has to accurately assess and deliver immediate patient care. In addition, she must have good communication skills to educate the patients and their families to follow the doctor's orders. She could give concrete instances in which she demonstrated all of these skills and got good results.

The nurse also used in her interview the fact that she took the initiative to take a sales course at night to learn how to apply her nursing skills to a sales position. This also demonstrated that she was self-motivated and wanted to understand the sales process. She landed the second sales position she ever applied for.

Another way to demonstrate to an interviewer that you are working to develop the required skills is to attend sales seminars and training classes like the ones listed in Chapter Five. It should be referred to frequently. Attending courses such as these lends credit to your resume and credence to your interview. A common complaint of sales managers is that most entry-level candidates do not read sales books or bother to take sales courses. The more courses taken and books read, the more prepared you will be for that first position, and the more you will stand out from other candidates in your interview.

Although the books listed in Chapter Five can help you develop the skills necessary to sell, other books can help you specifically with interviewing skills. Below are several of the best interviewing books for sales candidates.

- *Knock 'Em Dead.* Martin Yates. (Bob Adams, Inc.)
- *101 Great Answers to the Toughest Interview Questions.* Ron Fry. (Career Press.)
- *The Complete Q & A Job Interview Book.* Jeffrey G. Allen, JD. (CPC.)

GAUGING THE INTERVIEWING MANAGER'S EXPERIENCE

When preparing for an interview, it's also important to know something about the manager who will be interviewing you. The more you can find out about his past experience as a sales manager, the more informed you'll be on how he is thinking. If he has had formal training, for instance, you are more likely to be able to answer his questions the way he wants based on his background. Less experienced managers require different strategies. Before we discuss how to use knowledge of the manager's background to your advantage, however, we must discuss the kind of knowledge that is important to have in order to gauge the experience-level of your interviewer.

Managers who have never attended a seminar or read a book about prudent hiring practices can be classified as inexperienced.

Managers who have read a book or a few articles on how to hire salespeople are moderately experienced. Managers who are well informed, who have hired many previous reps, and who have read books and attended seminars on the right way to hire salespeople are very experienced and probably easier to prepare for.

Here are a few more questions to consider: How long has the manager been a sales manager? A week, month or year will indicate he may not have much experience. How many sales representatives has he hired during his time as a sales manager? Why did he hire these sales reps? Some hire based on personality or likeability. Has he had to replace any of these reps? Although he may have liked them, they may have been a poor choice for the position. These are the questions you should be asking before entering the interviewing process.

Oftentimes you can come right out and ask a manager these questions, but if you find it out beforehand you will be better prepared. In Chapters Nine and Eleven you will learn how to perform research on your target company and your interviewing sales managers. Talking with a sales rep in the company can also help you uncover helpful information. Ask a rep who works in the manager's division how that manager interviews. To find out what makes this manager tick, you need to know what personality traits he is looking for and what kinds of people he responds well to.

Don't Tell Them What You Think They Want to Hear

Many sales candidates answer questions based on what they *think* the manager wants to hear. The successful few answer interview questions based instead on what they *know* he wants to hear.

Successful interviewees read books not only on how to be a good interviewee, but also on how to be a good interviewer. For example, one consumer sales representative who was trying to find an entry-level position questioned several sales managers on what books they read and what courses and seminars they took to learn how to interview. He then read the books and obtained brochures and information on the seminars and courses that these managers had taken. "After reading these books," he said, "I no longer gave the answers that I wanted to give but rather the answers I *knew* the managers wanted to hear." The manager was happy because he was hiring the candidate that fit his profile. The candidate was happy because he had educated himself and had taken the time to understand what the manager really wanted in a sales representative.

Below is a list of books that can be found in the library or bookstore. These books instruct managers on good sound hiring practices. These books are all aimed at one thing: Educating managers on making the right hire the first time around. Many interviewing managers you will encounter will have read one or more of these books or even taken courses or seminars on how to hire sales representatives. Reading one or two of the books yourself will not only give you insight into good interviewing tactics, but also will give you more knowledge than most entry-level sales candidates you will be competing with.

- *Sales Managers Desk Book*. Gene Garofalo. (Prentice Hall.) Chapter Five, "How to Find and Hire Salespeople Who Can Sell," starts on page 70.
- *Hiring the Best: A Manager's Guide to Effective Interviewing*. Martin Yates. (Bob Adam, Inc.)
- *The Smart Interviewer: Tools and Techniques for Hiring the Best*. Bradford D. Smart. (John Wiley & Sons.)
- *How to Become a Skillful Interviewer*. Randi Toler Sachs. (AMACOM, The Work Smart Series.)
- *Ask the Headhunter*, by Nicholas Corcodilos. (Plum.) Though hard to find in stores, it can be ordered by calling 908-236-8440.

LESS EXPERIENCED MANAGERS

Interviewing with a less experienced manager is different than dealing with an experienced manager. With experienced managers, you may be able to gauge what criteria he used with candidates before you or find out from one of his reps what landed him the position. With a new sales manager, one who may have just been promoted from a sales position, there is no track record to examine. You may have to work harder on this type of interview and ask more probing questions. Instead of focusing on his management style, you may have to focus on his selling style and what made him successful. Often managers try to hire reps with styles similar to their own, especially if they were successful and are promoted from sales to management. You can use this to your advantage by giving him an example of how you would work the territory like he did.

> "Success is turning knowledge into positive action."
>
> Dorothy Leeds, author

For example, you find out from a rep who worked with your interviewing manager that he wrote follow-up letters to all his customers and that he felt this was a major contributing factor in his increased sales numbers. Then you may emphasize in the interview that you feel that follow-up is the most important thing you can do after the sales call, that you minored in journalism, and that you have great writing skills.

Finding information on the people you interview with will arm you with valuable insight. You will know what kind of traits to focus on and emphasize, and you will have time to come up with concrete examples of how you have exemplified those traits.

PERSONALITY TESTS

Many companies require as a condition of the interview that candidates take personality tests to see if a candidate actually fits the company mold. In the often bizarre questions that these tests ask, managers are looking not for specific answers, but for themes.

Some examples of what they are testing for are courage, ego, competition, focus, empathy, woo, communications, stamina, work order, sophistication, beliefs, and ethics.

Taking the test honestly is the recommendation most commonly given. They are testing to see if you are right for the position, whether you fit the profile that has been targeted for that particular position. It is also recommended that you are relaxed, that you schedule the interview when you've had a good night's sleep and are not distracted. It's also recommended that you take the test where it is quiet and where you can be alone. If possible, schedule the test during the time of day when you are at your best.

"[Pre-employment tests must be] predictive or significantly correlated with important elements of work behavior which comprise or are relevant to the job or jobs for which candidates are being evaluated."

U.S. Supreme Court, Albenarle Paper Co. vs. Moody (1975)

9

Knowing What to Ask:
Researching a Company Before
an Interview

By now you may have determined which industry you are targeting as an entry-level job candidate, and you may have an idea of how you will fit into that specific industry. You may have even identified your niche market and found out whether employment opportunities exist. Hopefully your target industry complements your background and you've taken steps to strengthen the match by developing the specific kinds of skills particular companies are seeking. You are becoming the ideal person a company is searching for—a candidate who has developed the necessary skills for selling, and more importantly, who can relate to the customers within its industry. The goal of an interview is to show a company that you are well matched to it in terms of general background and specific skills. To accomplish this goal you will need to have identified the particular company's general and specific needs, and you

> "I'm turned off by people who haven't done their homework."
>
> *Donald Kendall,*
> *chairman, PepsiCo.*

must be able to articulate how your skills and background are suited to those needs.

That is why, before going on an interview, you should know as much about your target company as any sales rep already employed by the company. On any given interview you could be asked to provide an impromptu status report about the company, its stock price, or information on any current event that may have involved or affected the company. Candidates who go to interviews without extensively researching such topics may stumble through the interview at a loss for words or may appear disorganized and insecure when asked these questions. Being unprepared can knock you out of the running for the position. If you do your homework before your interview by obtaining basic information such as product literature and financial statistics, this will not be the case.

> "My best advice for dealing with destructive anxiety is homework ... homework helps enormously when you apply for a job."
>
> Barbara Walters

Imagine walking into an interview and hearing the manager ask, "Why do you want to work for our company?" Your response should sound like this:

> "Your field has always piqued my interest, and that's why I decided to make a career change from my current field to sales. I've known this was my target industry for more than two years, and I've performed research on all the companies in this industry. I have literature, annual reports, Moody's Company Data Reports, and trade journals. In addition, I've read about and analyzed both your company and the competition. Your company had the best year in sales with the release of your three new products. I read an article in the recent issue of *Business Week* that stated that market analysts project your company will take fifteen to twenty percent of the market share points away from your largest competitor and become the leader in the next three to five years.
>
> "I've gained sales experience making sales calls, organizing sam-

ples, and typing marketing plans and sales forecasts when I recently rode with a sales rep for two days to gain more insight into selling. I have a letter he wrote outlining my experiences and recommending me as an excellent entry-level candidate for a sales position.

"The buyer, at one of your major accounts, Mr. Gladstone, and the other store managers whom I met while riding with the rep recommended I interview for this position. They were all very helpful when I contacted them afterward, requesting their help for my interview. I called on each one and asked them to help me obtain updated literature and pricing from your product's competitors and to answer my customer survey. When I commit to doing something, I like to be thorough and do the best job possible."

By responding with this answer, you demonstrate competence, enthusiasm, and interest in the position. This response will get you a high score with any evaluative criteria, but your main goal is to sound like you are an experienced sales person already, even if you have never sold prior to your interview.

> "There are no lazy veteran lion hunters."
>
> *Randall Douglas*

The best interviews are not simply question and answer sessions but are more like conversations between you and the interviewer. Not only must you be able to offer responses like the one described above, but you must also be knowledgeable enough to ask informed and intelligent questions. In short, you must know enough about the industry, company, and product to carry on an intelligent conversation with the interviewer.

Luck comes from preparation.

INDUSTRY LITERATURE

The most common way to polish these conversational skills is to read the *Wall Street Journal*, *USA Today*, and other weekly periodicals, business newspapers, magazines, and trade journals—especially publications in which your target company places advertisements. You will find out who is reducing their offshoot companies, what is happening with various brand names, which are companies' best selling brands, what their sales strategies are, and whether the industry may be cutting back or growing. If the company is publicly traded, look at the stock price and history of the stock. If the stock recently went up or down, find out why.

"If you want to know a good company's shared values, just look at its annual report."

John Stewart

Reading will inform you of what is going on in the industry and you will be able to carry on a conversation that will demonstrate this knowledge. As the above interview response revealed, these topics are also excellent subjects for opening remarks that will impress an interviewing manager. Performing research through reading will give you knowledge that will help you not only at your interview, but also throughout your career.

CONTACTING COMPANIES DIRECTLY

You can also obtain vital information directly from your target company itself. For practice obtaining such information, call various companies and ask for information about their products, sales literature, pricing, and financial statistics. Company employees from the customer service department to the president's secretary are used to receiving these types of inquiries. You may, however, have to be creative in your approach to obtaining this information. Most companies when contacted will send literature, including financial information, to potential customers, current customers, or individuals looking to make an investment in that company. You may have to use the old term paper technique, or say that you are a potential new customer or investor. Which approach is appropriate will depend on your particular situation and what kind of information you are requesting. You may have to make several attempts to obtain the information, so plan ahead.

Always remember to be organized and to develop a list of questions before contacting anyone. Keep files for the companies you're interested in, and list the features and benefits of their products. The gathered literature and financial reports will give you a profile of what the companies sell, how well they are performing financially, and how they market and sell their products. Contact their competitors and obtain the same information so you can compare them and be aware of everyone's place in the market.

PRODUCT DEVELOPMENT MANAGERS

In addition to requesting literature from a company, asking to speak with someone in product development or product management may also be helpful. One sales rep tells the following story of her search for a position in medical sales. This is an excellent example of how research among product managers can provide key information that can make you the best prepared job candidate.

Because she would be interviewing for a position where she had an enormous amount of competition, she needed to know more than what the customers told her and what was in the literature, financial report, and library publications—something no one else would know. She developed a list of questions a buyer would ask by asking the customers what they needed to know in order to buy a product. She then called her interviewing company and its competitors and asked for the product manager for the medical devices she hoped to sell. Since this person was responsible for that particular product, she knew he would have vital information pertaining to any new products or feature enhancements. She told them she was a customer making a buying decision, and asked him why his product was superior to the competition and why she should buy his product instead of the competition.

Then, she asked a couple of the competitors' managers and sales reps questions such as how they viewed her target company and whether it was a true contender in the market. The managers were complimentary of the company and told her she would be making an excellent career move. They told her that the company was one of the top three and that they all really had to compete for the business.

Using the information she had gathered, she delivered a sales presentation to the manager during her interview outlining why their product was superior to the competition. She used the literature and the sample questions and answers, and she made a competitive grid with all of the products listed. She typed the information on a graph with the features and benefits of the company she was interviewing with and those of its competitors. Then she described how the interviewer's product would soon be adding two extra features. She also had information on which new features would be added to the competitive products' in the next six months. The manager hadn't known the competition was changing their product, and he really appreciated her research. She impressed the manager so much that he flew her to the home office within two days for a final interview, and she landed the job.

CUSTOMER-BASED RESEARCH

If you can't obtain the information directly from the company, contact a customer of the company and explain that you're in the process of interviewing and would like information on all of the companies. The story of one job candidate looking for a position in the ski apparel industry provides an excellent example of a customer-oriented research strategy.

This candidate went to several ski shops and asked each of the store managers to order additional catalogs and information on the companies they did business with. He gleaned all the information he needed before the interview from the managers and the bonus literature, including the competitors' pricing, catalogs, and a customer survey that he gave to each of the store managers. He became familiar with the different lines, the price points, and the target customers for each line of ski clothing. He found out why the buyer for the ski shop would order each different ski outfit for his store. He knew what would sell and what wouldn't sell from the line of apparel he would be representing and why. His extensive research among the store managers not only prepared him for his interview, but also built the valuable relationships a rep needs with his clients.

CUSTOMER SURVEYS

Contacting the customer is the best form of research you can do to gain inlight about the company, past representatives, service, competition, and the sales potential of the customers themselves. Never skip this step. However, when talking with customers and clients, be careful not to give away any sensitive or insider information about your target company or position—that could lead to difficulties between the two companies. To be as safe as possible, keep your customer surveys free from a focus on just one business or position.

The list below provides sample questions to ask a customer when you make contact to perform research for the interview.

What does it take for a business to be successful?
"The secret of any business is to understand the customer's problems and to provide solutions so as to help them be profitable and feel good about the transaction."

Francis G. "Buck" Rodgers, IBM

- Which manufacturers do you purchase these particular products from?
- How many companies manufacture these products?
- Why do you buy from the companies you mentioned and not the others?
- Did you ever buy products from other companies who sell the same or similar products in the past?
- If yes, why did you stop? If no, why didn't you buy their product?
- How long does it take from the time you are introduced to a product until you order it?
- What is the process you go through in deciding to actually purchase a product?
- What is the average purchase quantity of this product? In dollars?
- How quickly do these products sell to your customers or get used by your company?
- Which companies do you feel do the best job at marketing their products?
- What particular services do you expect from a sales rep when he calls on you?
- Do your current sales reps meet these expectations? Would you buy more of one product from a company who provided a particular service?
- How has the service from the previous rep rated compared to the other two companies you buy from?
- Can you give me the names and numbers of the competitive sales reps?
- If you were to sell for a company, which one would you want to work for?
- Which trade shows or conventions do you attend?
- What trade journals or publications do you read?
- Where are advertisements placed for your business's products?

This is a generic list of sample questions. It is by no means exhaustive. There may be questions you should know in order to be prepared for a particular interview that aren't listed, so as you look for a position in your target industry, make a list of things you must know and develop your own list of questions.

Once you've made your list, call at least five customers and ask them your questions. Then, take these responses and type these surveys to use on your interview. As you become somewhat familiar with the reputations and sales histories of the various brand names, and with the customer base who will buy the product or service from a company, you'll find it easier to conduct intelligent conversations on your interview.

PREVIOUS SALES REPS

Reps will give you insight into a company in a way that no other person possibly could, especially if you can find the reps who previously worked your targeted territory. Let's say the rep you want to replace had been in the territory for two years, but you're having trouble contacting him or even finding out his name. Look for this information from the company's customers. You find out from a store buyer that the leaving rep's name is Stan Williams and the rep before him was Bruce Jones. Contact both of

> Believe one who
> has tried it.
>
> *Virgil*

these reps before the interview. Bruce will probably be able to give you more unbiased insight into the company than will Stan. Although you may be able to pick up valuable information from the attitude of either rep, Stan, not wanting to upset his current manager, may be more diplomatic than Bruce. He may say something like, "That manager is a great guy, and it is a great entry-level position for training, but once you have two years under your belt, another company will probably steal you away with a great offer you cannot pass up. By the way, the manager loves to talk about football and is an avid golfer." Bruce, on the other hand, because he has been away from the job longer, may say, "Oh, another one bites the dust. That manager cannot keep a rep for more than two years. He just grinds 'em up." Stan's information may be helpful, but Bruce's will probably be more candid and insightful.

Besides knowing that the manager likes sports, reps posses a wealth of inside gossip that you can use to your advantage. Chapter Eleven will discuss in more detail how to use inside gossip and will warn you more extensively about the pitfalls of not talking with insiders of a company. But here are a couple of the important questions to consider for now: What if the company is having problems and all of the current reps are bailing out? What if the commissions have been cut and quotas are being raised to unreasonable levels? I can promise you that neither *The Wall Street Journal* nor *USA Today* will report these news flashes. Only a current sales rep can warn you of such red flags.

TRADE SHOWS

Remember that attending trade shows and conventions is another resource for learning and finding literature about the industry in which you want to gain employment. Companies have products on display, and they sometimes use these shows to introduce a new product or conduct research for new products. By attending these shows, you'll be able to make face-to-face contact with a representative of the company. You may be able to ask for demonstrations of products or presentations. Such information could be valuable on an interview. Always take a note pad and pen to jot down notes as you make your rounds to each of the companies' booths. These notes will help you when you prepare for an interview.

Make sure you collect the exhibit books at the convention and pick up as much literature as possible. The exhibit books contain a directory of the companies exhibiting, along with their addresses, phone numbers, and product listings. When you land that interview, use this book as a reference to start your research phone calls as quickly as possible.

CHAMBERS OF COMMERCE

Another common research avenue is calling the Chamber of Commerce in your city for background information on your company. Each chamber has a "Business and Industry Journal," as well as a "Population and Employment Overview." Obtain further information by contacting the chamber in the city where your target company has its home office.

However, the only way to find out this information from most Chambers of Commerce is to either join the chamber or find an existing member who may obtain this information for you. Some chambers, however, may send it to you without joining—you'll just have to test the waters. Whether you go to visit the chamber on your own or attend the chamber meetings, it is worth the trip to research what they have on record. Often one chamber is able to contact another chamber office to obtain the information you're seeking.

OUTPLACEMENT FIRMS AND CAREER COUNSELORS

If you are working with an outplacement firm or career counselor, use them as another excellent source of information. If you contact an outplacement firm, ask whether it has access to "Moody's Company Data Reports," which provides the following information:

- The location of a company.
- The exchange the company is traded on.
- The principal lines of business it is in.
- The financial information and history of a company.
- What companies it has acquired and sold, as well as joint ventures it has formed with other companies.
- Information on the products, marketing, research and development, properties, subsidiaries, management, directors, auditors, rating, capital stock, and an Annual Income Statement.

The information is all in this one conclusive report. If you can get a hold of it, you can save research time in the library.

OTHER SOURCES

Books like *Knock 'em Dead* by Martin Yates (Bob Adams, Inc.) and *How You Really Get Hired* by John L. LaFevre (ARCO) are excellent books that provide additional advice on how to perform research.

Also, don't forget to search your file of contacts for people who may be able to provide additional information for your interview. All of the information you've gathered by making contacts with reps and managers can help you build a powerful presentation for your interview. Remember that recruiters, too, are excellent sources for background information on different companies.

Never stop reaching for more.

> "Do more than exist—live.
> Do more than touch—feel.
> Do more than look—observe.
> Do more than read—listen.
> Do more than listen—understand."
>
> John H. Rhoades

KNOWING WHAT TO ASK

Doing your homework before entering the interviewing arena can make you appear more experienced than you may actually be. The overview of a company and its products that you gain from your research will not only help you answer interview questions intelligently and knowledgeably, but it'll also help you develop a list of intelligent questions to ask

> *"A genius is a talented person who does his homework."*
>
> *Thomas Edison*

your interviewer in return. Asking questions gives you the opportunity to convey your enthusiasm, your knowledge of the company and the industry, and most importantly, to gain insight into your interviewing manager. Below is a list of questions to ask at an interview that can supplement those you develop through your research.

INTERVIEWING YOUR INTERVIEWING MANAGER

- What is your background?
- How long have you been with the company?
- Describe your management style.
- Why did you choose to work for this company?
- How would you describe a typical day in the field in this territory?
- How often and how closely do you work with the sales reps?
- How do you evaluate the sales reps after you work with them?

FINDING OUT WHAT THE MANAGER WANTS

- What qualities would the ideal candidate for this position possess?
- What is the most important quality you are looking for in a candidate?

- How many sales reps have you hired in the last two to three years? Why did you hire those reps?
- How many sales reps does your company currently have or plan to have?

TENURE AND RANK OF SALES REPS IN THE COMPANY

- How long has the most senior rep been with the company?
- How many sales reps have been in this territory over the past five years? How long did each rep work the territory?
- How successful were they in the territory? Where did he or she rank among the other reps in the company?
- How many of the sales reps made quota last year?
- What was the income of the highest paid sales rep? The lowest?

QUESTIONS ABOUT THE TERRITORY

- What is the geography of this territory?
- How does the territory rank within the company?
- What is the current dollar volume of the territory?
- What is the quota per month or year for this territory?
- How are quotas set?
- Compared to this company's number one territory what is this territory's market share versus the competition's market share?

SALES TRAINING QUESTIONS

- What type of training do sales reps go through at your company?
- How long is the training?
- What is the learning curve for the average sales rep?

QUESTIONS ABOUT THE COMPANY ITSELF

- Where do you see the company in one year? In three years? Five?
- How much of the company's revenues are devoted to marketing?
- Does the company generally promote from within?
- How does the company honor its commitments (i.e. to customers, employees, etc.)?

QUESTIONS ABOUT THE SALES CYCLE

- What is the average sales cycle for this company's products?
- What is the most difficult part of the sales cycle?
- How long has a particular product been on the market?
- With new competitors coming into the market, what strategy does the company have to maintain and grow its market share?

QUESTIONS TO FIND OUT IF YOU ARE GOING TO BE ASKED BACK FOR A SECOND INTERVIEW

- After this interview today, do you feel I have the qualities you are looking for?
- Do I fit the mold? Would I be a good fit for this position?
- Where do I rank in regard to other candidates for this position?
- What do I need to do in order to be your number one candidate?
- When will be the next scheduled interview?
- When will you make your final decision on who you will hire for this territory?

These are only examples of the kinds of questions to ask an interviewing manager. Add to the list depending on the particular company or type of position. Through your research, you may already know many of the answers to these questions, but it may still be a good idea to ask them just to learn more about your interviewing manager. Not only are these kinds of questions important in demonstrating your knowledge and enthusiasm, but their answers are vital to know before you accept any sales position.

Depending on how much time you have and what stage of the interviewing process you're in, there may be other questions you'll want to ask. If there are three interviews, you may want to pick one or two questions from each of the sections above for each interview, or you may cover different individual categories at each interview. If required to interview with several people within one company, you'll want to compile separate lists of questions appropriate for each individual. Your interviewer may even inform you that he'll be conducting the interviews in stages and ask you to reserve certain questions for a particular time. Still, before accepting any position, be sure that you've had the opportunity to get all the answers you need.

ANTICIPATE QUESTIONS

Not only is it important to have a list of questions prepared to ask your interviewing manager, but it is also helpful to prepare a list of questions you think the manager will ask you. One sales rep I knew applied the "Ben Duffy Method" on his interview. Ben Duffy was a sales rep who prepared a list of ten questions before each sales call. The questions were not questions to ask a customer, but questions he anticipated the customer would ask *him*. Then on each call he would give the list to the customer and ask whether these were the questions he was about to ask. This type of planning projected an image that Duffy was genuinely prepared to meet the customer's needs. Using Duffy's idea, this rep prepared a list of ten questions he thought the manager would ask and gave it to him at the interview. He had researched enough about interviewing techniques to feel confident that his questions would closely match the interviewer's. Needless to say he had the perfect answers rehearsed, and of course, he landed the job. Before interviewing, anticipate the interviewer's questions and rehearse their answers. Even if you do not give the interviewer your list, your preparation will still help you shine.

RESEARCHING A COMPANY WITH LIMITED TIME

If you are under a time restraint for preparing for the interview, here are three methods of getting the information in a crunch. Try to use the latest services and technologies available.

- Obtain a Federal Express or UPS account number. It costs nothing to obtain a number, and you will have it available when you need it. If you have to prepare for an interview quickly, use the number to have information sent overnight to you.
- Having access to a fax machine, or at least a fax number at your nearest twenty-four-hour Kinko's or copy center, is a necessity. If you have an 8:00 A.M. interview the next day, you can ask your source to fax you the most vital information. For any interview you need at least the fundamental information about the company. A fax number is also important once you are working as a sales rep, so it may make sense to get one now.
- Internet access and an email address can be extremely helpful in researching companies' web sites and sending and receiving information quickly. If you are not on-line, perhaps you have a friend or neighbor who is.

As interviewing events accelerate, you will need to be able to retrieve documents quickly, instead of stopping momentum to perform research. Keep well-organized files of information, and document all of your research. Organization is one of the skills a

> What we have to learn to do, we learn by doing.
>
> *Aristotle*

company will look for, so begin developing this skill now. You should also practice researching companies in advance so that when you do land an interview, you will know the steps.

DRESSING FOR THE OCCASION

One final bit of research you must perform before the interview is wardrobe shopping. In any interview, looking the part is half the battle. As an experienced sales professional, I always instruct both

> "Most people who fail to get the job they really want fail not because they are not qualified but because they failed in the interview. And most failure occurs because they aren't prepared."
>
> *David W. Crawley, Jr.*

men and women to look at what other sales reps are wearing in the industry. Appropriate dress can vary from pin-stripe suits to dress casual to active wear. If you're looking for a position in the apparel industry, try to wear something from the interviewer's line.

Another good strategy is to use a personal shopper. Go to a couple of department stores near your home and set up an appointment with at least two personal shoppers. Explain that you are on a budget,

but you need a couple of interview suits, preferably on sale. Mention that once you have a job you will return because you will need a wardrobe. Because she probably works off of commissions, too, this relationship can be beneficial to both of you.

Also, personal shoppers may be able to give you information about outlet stores. Neiman Marcus, for example, has a store called "Last Call," which has discounted suits for men and women. Outlet stores are great for people on a budget, even though you may have to really hunt through the racks.

150

10

Winning the Job: Preparing a Marketing Strategy to Present at the Interview

BESIDES KNOWING THE RIGHT QUESTIONS TO ASK, A sales rep candidate must prove to his interviewer that he has the ability to research and organize to set goals and can create and implement the strategies to achieve them. Arriving at the interview with a well-researched marketing strategy in hand is the best way to demonstrate these skills to an interviewer. You should have enough information from your research to develop this marketing strategy and win the job.

> "I can't imagine a person becoming a success who doesn't give this game of life everything he's got."
>
> *Walter Cronkite*

ASK OTHER REPS

When initially taking over a territory, new sales reps will either have to develop a sales strategy or follow one that has been prepared for them by the company—usually reps have to reach sales goals set by their managers. Each industry, territory, and company may be different, so you must determine the best way to develop such a strategy for your situation. A new rep must work off of records, leads, and computer sheets. If such records are absent, then it becomes his job to create them. A rep will also need to prepare projections for how many units he'll need to sell each month to make his quota and to develop strategies for landing new business and meeting these projections. If you can't do this on your own, then call the sales reps you've made contact with and ask them what they would do (and have done) to develop an effective sales strategy. Take advantage of the knowledge and ingenuity of your contacts. Sales reps take over new territories all the time and all must perform the rituals described in this chapter. The ones who have a well-organized method will be the most successful.

What is a Marketing Strategy?

Every company has had, at one time or another, to develop a comprehensive business plan to make sales projections, set goals, borrow money, and make formal presentations to stockholders and board members.

> A good marketing strategy is one that keeps what you have and gets what you don't have.
>
> *Sarro*

If you look in the business section of any bookstore, there are lots of books on how to write business plans. A marketing strategy is akin to a business plan, just shorter in scope. It functions the same and should be just as well thought out as a five-year business plan is for a major corporation. A rep's marketing strategy is important to a sales manager, because it is a part of the manager's own larger strategy for reaching the company's sales projections for his division. The manager's strategy is designed to meet goals outlined in an even broader business plan that he has developed or that has been passed down to him from upper management. A sales manager needs to know that you are capable of running the territory the way he needs you to in order to meet his own goals.

In addition to formal marketing strategies, or as a supplement to them, managers request from sales reps weekly and monthly itineraries, and monthly, quarterly, and annual sales reports. Managers also request information on how many units a customer will buy, the number of units used by the customer in a month or quarter, competitive information on usage or purchases, and the projected time between a planned sales call and a sale (sales cycle). Most often these requests come in the form of a memo from a sales manager sent by fax, e-mail, intercompany mail, or voice mail.

When you receive that memo that says, "A business plan or territory overview explaining how you are going to reach you sales goals for the next year is due by next Friday," you don't want to waste time figuring out how to write a report. By preparing one now for your interviews, you'll have the knowledge and experience for the real thing.

DEVELOPING THE STRATEGY

To develop your initial marketing strategy, first envision yourself taking over a territory. Your strategy depends on the current condition of the territory. If your proposed territory is already productive, outline the steps necessary to keep the territory's positive momentum in an upward trend, i.e. increase sales. If you are about to inherit a territory that has been less than productive, you'll need to outline how you'll turn the territory around.

SAMPLE MARKETING STRATEGY

The following sample marketing strategy is an outline of what a sales rep does to understand his new territory's history. You can use it to take over a territory in a quick and organized fashion. The plan will show you how to:

- Obtain and format the necessary information.
- Describe the way the territory will be covered once you take over.
- Form strategies for developing existing accounts and targeting new ones.

The sample marketing strategy is a generic report that can be adapted to fit just about any territory's situation. The example provided is for a territory in which a previous sales representative has been working, there is an established customer base, there are current contracts that need to be reviewed and enforced, and target customers have been established by the previous sales rep.

MARKETING STRATEGY

FOR

(NAME OF COMPANY)

PREPARED FOR: (NAME OF SALES MANAGER)

BY

(YOUR NAME)

(DATE)

PROPOSED MARKETING STRATEGY

I. UNDERSTANDING THE PAST

- Review sales training materials and attend sales training classes.
- Learn features and benefits of product or service (*depending on your product line or industry, i.e., types of materials, colors, patterns, types of equipment, etc.*).
- Work with sales trainer (*if your company has one*) to learn how the company wants the territory run, including number of calls per day, how calls are to be scheduled, how sales presentations and demonstrations are to be made, how sales information is to be organized and reported, and other standard policies.
- Learn about competitors' products and information.

II. ORGANIZING THE TERRITORY

- Research and organize account records and files that the previous sales representative accumulated while working the territory.
- Review sales records and purchase orders for existing customers to analyze current status of territory in terms of number of units or sales dollars.
- Analyze computer printouts and sales records from previous year to current year to search for increases or decreases, loss or decline in usage of product or service, recent purchases, and increase or decrease in dollars spent with company.
- Develop new account profiles (computer or paper records) that thoroughly document pertinent information for each account. The profiles will maintain accurate and up-to-date information enabling the rep to work and adequately cover the territory (*describe the territory*). Territory consists of three states: Texas, Oklahoma, and Louisiana. Profiles will include contact names, titles, address, contact phone number, fax, voice mail, account number, product history, competition, call activity, quarterly

objectives, and yearly objectives. (*Some companies and managers make this mandatory, and sales reps are evaluated on territory record-keeping for merit increases and bonuses.*)

- Review all existing contracts, bids, and targets set by previous sales rep or sales manager.
- Determine whether contracts are being honored by the customer. Address any bid requests for accounts needing pricing or proposals. Evaluate validity of targets.
- Read previous sales rep's activity reports and notes, and contact previous sales rep if there are questions about the reports, records, or notes (*if rep left on good terms*).
- Schedule meetings with sales manager to discuss accounts that were being worked on prior to or during sales rep's departure from the company.
- Obtain any sales leads from customer service, previous sales rep, sales markets, and conventions or trade shows.
- Send out introductory letters announcing that a new sales representative is now taking over the territory.

III. CLAIMING THE PRESENT

- Call to schedule appointments with most recent inquiries, leads, and current accounts. Start calling where previous rep left off.
- Work first with accounts that require immediate attention and ensure all issues are addressed.
- Schedule appointments with other customers or sales leads in the same geographical area. On each appointment go over account profiles with customer to update records and ensure that we are working with accurate and updated data for each account.
- Visit each account to make personal introductions after introductory letters are sent to assess business opportunities, discover whether customer's needs are being met, and to ensure that all commitments from previous sales rep have been carried out.

IV. Planning the Future

- Evaluate previous rep's target accounts to judge whether sufficient sales can be generated to meet company goals.
- Set up weekly, monthly, and quarterly plans with room for revision.
- Target accounts in order of importance to establish weekly and monthly coverage plan.
- Divide territory into target areas for easier management. Divide territory into a call cycle of four, five, or six weeks to insure proper coverage of all key and target accounts.
- Identify an itinerary to accomplish monthly, quarterly, and year-end sales goals.
- Establish method of follow-up with each account: telephone, written correspondence, voice mail, or follow-up appointments and presentations.
- Use updated account information, inquiries, and requests for pricing, demonstrations, and appointments to revise previous sales reps targets and business plans.
- Work other accounts in area to gather data and develop new leads to budget time, travel, and coverage efficiently.
- Update manager on any pertinent information or discoveries when initially calling on accounts to make adjustments in quotas.

There may be many different scenarios for each position you interview for, and adjustments in the marketing strategy should be made accordingly. For example, the territory may not fit this description. It may be a brand new company, a different industry, or there may be an entirely new sales force. The position opening could be for a new or expanded territory, or you could be responsible for limited accounts or select accounts only. There may not be a previous sales representative, computer printouts, account records, profiles, or sales records. In these cases, you will have to be creative. Use different action verbs to describe each task, such as: Develop, create, establish, implement, launch, set up, or other applicable terms.

> "The very first step toward success in any job is to become interested in it."
>
> William Osler

With a thoughtful and organized market strategy, you'll be so prepared that even if it's your first interview for a sales position, you will come off as a bright, energetic candidate that the manager will want to hire. Remember, interviewing is all about winning—winning over the manager, making him feel that if he doesn't hire you, he's making the wrong decision. The excuse of "lack of sales experience" will start to disappear if you can demonstrate that you are knowledgeable, qualified, and enthusiastic.

11

Final Advice:
Avoiding Pitfalls and
Outwitting Sharks

THE PAST TEN CHAPTERS HAVE CONTAINED MANY EXAMPLES, details, and instructions for making contacts, gaining experience, and interviewing effectively so that you can land the sales job of your dreams. This chapter, however, will give you some insight on anticipating and overcoming some of the problems of actually being a sales rep. In any career, people are bound to encounter problems. Almost everyone, to some degree, will have to learn by trial and error. Luckily, many of these problems are common—almost every rep will see them at one time or another. I'm hoping that you can learn from the stories of the mistakes and mishaps told here, rather than having to experience every pitfall yourself. Without knowledge of the "sharks" and what other sales reps have done to outwit them, you won't be prepared. Or worse, you could needlessly make the same mistakes.

> "It's not whether you get knocked down. It's whether you get up again."
>
> *Vince Lombardi,*
> *football coach*

159

Through these examples you'll learn to think like a shark, anticipate potential pitfalls, and steer clear of negative situations. Sales managers will respect you more if you can outplay them at their game. Getting a job is one thing, but it is even more difficult finding and accepting the *right* job. You don't want to make mistake after mistake or hop from job to job. Mistakes can cost you money, and a loss of income can cause you to lose confidence in yourself. I don't mean to discourage you or test your confidence level. This is important information to help you navigate the potentially treacherous career waters more safely.

Many sales reps, including myself, have been through corporate downsizing, bad management, and bad products, and have often been misled by promises. Knowing what I know today, I do not trust anyone until he proves himself deserving of my trust. I have been through many shark-infested waters, and I have a few scars to show for it. I did not avoid the pitfalls; I fell right into them. I now have the benefit of personal hindsight as well as interviews with other sales professionals concerning their job searches. I was fortunate that with all of the things that happened in my career, I was able to pull myself together, find other positions, and use the information I gained from each experience to write this book. After all the pitfalls I've encountered, I've learned that you have to be really creative to stay afloat.

Do most sales reps stumble into the pitfalls? Not always. With a little luck, some manage to avoid the sharks unknowingly, or over time they learn to think like the sharks and outsmart them. Others watch their friends and colleagues go through bad situations, so they learn to ask more questions, thoroughly research the company, product, and management to gain insight into the types of people who work there. They get everything in writing.

When you start looking for a job, it is easy to begin feeling rejected and let down after getting a few rejection letters telling you that you're not right for the position. With each rejection, disheartening as it is, remember to focus on what you've just learned, evaluate what you've done wrong, and keep trying until you do it right. Some candidates take up to two or three years to finally land a position. Don't give up hope. With the information in this book, you have an advantage.

> "Accepting good advice increases one's own ability."
>
> Johann Wolfgang von Goethe

The following stories are warnings. Most sales rep positions are exciting and rewarding, however, there are common problems that can outweigh the benefits if they get out of hand. These examples will help you identify situations and positions to avoid *before* you're involved. Like many careers, a great start doesn't guarantee a great rest-of-the-career.

GAUGE THE TERRITORY'S STABILITY

A sales rep about to go on her final interview wanted to make a really good impression—she needed something that would give her an edge over the other candidates. She used the example of the marketing strategy found in Chapter Ten to develop one for her target company, but she went a step further and developed a customer survey as well. She wanted to understand what the previous sales rep had done in the territory and whether the customers felt the company and products were good. She surveyed ten key accounts and asked the following four questions to obtain the information she needed.

- Do you currently use this specific product?
- What other kinds of product do you use? Why?
- What is your overall impression of this specific company?
- What do you think of your sales rep?

Her responses were that seven of the ten accounts currently used the equipment, and seven named other vendors that they used. Overall, in customer satisfaction, four accounts rated their overall impression of the company as "Excellent," three rated the company as "Good," and one account rated the company as "Poor." (Two accounts had no opinion, because they had never used the product.) As for their impression of the sales rep, three accounts knew who he was and were satisfied, two accounts weren't sure who he was but thought they knew, and five accounts didn't know the rep at all. After her survey, she was confident that the product was good, but the fact that the rep was unknown in five of the ten accounts surprised her. This was excellent information about the territory for her final interview.

On her final interview in the home office, she gave everyone a copy of the marketing strategy and the survey. She won the job because she knew what was going on in the territory. Because there were no records from the previous rep, and because he had not worked the territory thoroughly, she knew it would take her some time to perform damage control. With this in mind, she negotiated a guaranteed commission for the first few months before accepting the position. A year and a half later she won an award for having the highest increase in the country. This is a wonderful example of how taking over a bad territory can prove to be advantageous—the only way your numbers can go is up.

> A problem is a chance for you to do your best.
>
> *Duke Ellington*

MANAGEMENT CHANGES

This story, however, does have a downside. Soon after her first year on the job, her manager was promoted. She ended up with a new sales manager who wanted to put a friend of his in her position. He made her life a living hell, even though her numbers were great and she was selling more and more each month. Dealing with a new manager in midstream proved disastrous to her career, and she ended up leaving the company. This story is told by many sales reps. Disagreeable new sales managers are a fact of life that many reps encounter often.

Another sales rep was hired for a sales territory that was at the bottom of the rankings. She was so excited just to get the job that she felt confident she could turn the territory around. She worked very hard with her manager, who soon became her mentor. She went from last to first place in one year, was awarded Rookie of the Year, and was number one in sales training. Then the dreaded day came—her manager was promoted, and she had lost her mentor.

The manager who replaced her mentor was a "good ole boy" who wanted an all-boys' team. He put on the pressure and made himself impossible to work for. Because she didn't have the right anatomy, she soon left the position. Within three days of her resignation, her new manager had a replacement—a "good ole boy."

Unfortunately, problems arising from changes in management are all too common. If at all possible, avoid taking a position where the manager may get promoted within the near future. But usually you won't find this out until you're with the company a year or more, but it doesn't hurt to ask a few questions up front. Be direct— this is important. Ask, "What would happen if I took this position and a year from now you get promoted. I've heard of instances where the new manager comes in and wants his own team." If you find out the manager is looking for a promotion, you can discuss your concerns further once you have the offer.

If you do wind up with a new manager shortly after taking a job, try to shine. Let him know how much you enjoy working with the company and that you are a team player. If conflict does arise, the best advice is to not try to fight him—you will lose. Try to reason with him, and do everything he asks, because he holds all the cards.

Whatever you do, go into the transition with an open mind. You never know, you could actually end up liking the new manager more. One rep told me he was happy his old manager was promoted because he tended to micro-manage. The new, more hands-off manager felt like a blessing.

EVALUATE THE CHARACTER OF THE COMPANY

Another gentleman, the inventor of bar codes, advises job-seekers to know the answers to the following five things before joining any company:

- What is your management-to-employee ratio?
- Do you promote from within?
- Are your promotions based on merit?
- What is the level of stability and the debt-to-earning ratio?
- How well do you feel your company follows up on its commitments to people within and outside the organization?

The answers to these questions can help you evaluate the stability of a company, your chances for advancement, whether you will be overmanaged, and how commitments are respected. If management gives skewed or unsatisfactory answers to these questions, this is probably not the best company to work for.

THE DREADED "INTERNAL CANDIDATE"

Occaisionally, even though you've scrupulously followed every single step in this book, wowed 'em in the interview, and even been called back for another meeting, a sales manager will pass you over for a candidate from inside the company. Be prepared, this dreaded

internal candidate pops up from nowhere, and nine times out of ten
he gets the job. A referral from inside keeps you more informed
than most other applicants, but those internal candidates can be
tricky to predict. Ask the manager up front if there are any internal
candidates, especially if he starts asking for dates when you can go
to the home office. At least if you know ahead of time, you will
keep looking and keep your options open. Don't stop looking for
job openings until you receive a formal offer in writing.

COMMISSION SWINDLING

One sales rep, George, told a horror story of being swindled out of
his hard-earned commission by his manager. His immediate supervisor was a great guy, but the regional manager was notorious for
waiting until the end of the year and then
changing the quotas so he would not have
to pay the reps all of their commissions. At
the sales reps' January meeting, the rep
asked the regional manager whether his
calculation was correct for his commission.
The regional manager looked him in the

> "When power is in the
> hands of men it will be
> sometimes abused."
>
> *Samuel Johnson*

eye and said, "I can't pay you that much commission. You do like
your job, don't you?" A few days later a memo came from the manager saying:

> "George, I would like to confirm our conversation at the recent area
> meeting regarding your targets. In light of the recent product
> loading on this product, you suggested your adjusted plan be
> dropped and the original plan be used to compute your final payout.
> George, this will be done per your request.
> "George, I would like to comment on your request and the spirit
> in which it was made. It is evidence that it is still possible for people
> to deal with each other in a fair manner. Personally, it was very
> refreshing and I appreciate very much what you have done."

Obviously, George had done nothing of the kind. The manager had simply and unabashedly cheated him out of his hard earned commissions. Because this was George's first position, he didn't want to fight the manager because he needed a good reference. Instead, George took the only other available option—he left the company. He rightly supposed that if this manager had cheated him once, he would do it over and over again. Unfortunately, the manager *did* cheat reps frequently, because he knew he could get away with it. Had George found out beforehand by talking to other reps who worked for this manager, he could have discussed his findings on his interview with his direct supervisor. Before accepting the position he could have had something written in his acceptance letter stating that no adjustments could be made to his commissions when he earned them. If the company didn't agree to these terms, George would not have accepted this one year stint that now stands out like a sore thumb on his resume.

FALLING PRICE CURVES

Another new rep, Michael, took over a territory that had been the number one territory during the previous year. He was excited because the territory was doing great and still bringing in large monthly commissions. At the time he took over the territory his product was selling for one hundred dollars per unit. He had eighty percent of his business in twenty percent of his accounts, which usually is the rule in sales. In short, everything seemed to be in great shape.

One day, however, Michael got a call from a customer who complained that his pricing was too high. A competitor's product of almost equal quality had begun selling for only fifty dollars. When his competition began courting his top accounts by undercutting his price, Michael was overwhelmed and didn't know what to do.

His response to the customer was that the two products were not of the same quality, but several accounts threatened to switch to the other supplier. Michael's manager refused to lower the prices. "Sell quality," he kept saying. Michael argued with his sales manager that the customers were going to switch to the other product, but he wouldn't lower the prices. He had to argue with his manager daily to drop the pricing—and he always lost. He had to sell more to other new accounts to make up the difference in dollars lost with the other accounts. After two years he quit.

Exhausted by this experience, Michael now always asks questions about the Actual Sales Price, if it is dropping or remaining the same. Many products, once they reach a point in the marketing phase, begin to drop. You want to come into a product while it's on the left side of the marketing curve and still growing, not after it's topped off and is falling to the right. This is a common hazard in any market, and management has to adjust the commission structures and quotas to compensate, or the company has to have a pipeline of new products to make up for the effects of market saturation. Inflexibility in management to see this problem is a troublesome pitfall to overcome.

GET IT IN WRITING

Anytime someone makes you an offer, get everything in writing. If the company refuses to put it in writing, refuse to take the position no matter how badly you want the job. One rep took a position for the stock options. The management team told her that she would get five thousand shares of stock, vesting twenty-five percent each year on her anniversary. A few months later in a sales meeting, the president handed out the stock options. He instructed everyone to hurry, sign them, and return them. When she flipped to the vesting date, it was not the date that had been promised. It was seven months later. She knew at that moment she'd been had. Not wanting to draw attention to herself, she reluctantly signed the options. A few months later the entire sales force was let go. She realized that there had never been any intention of giving the reps the options. Get it in writing. It keeps everyone honest. This applies to everything: Salaries, commissions, benefits, guarantees, car allowances, or company car offers. Never begin a job with any company without a formal offer letter, and never resign from a current employer until you have a written offer from the new company. The risk is real that you could find yourself unemployed.

CONSIDER PERSONAL COMPATIBILITY

Finding a good manager is just like finding a mate. You don't know a person until you spend time with him. Personal relationships and relationships on the job have a lot in common. Everything can be going great for the first few months, and then you can find out that the relationship is not really what you thought it was. Or you may find what seems like perfect match for you only to discover they do not feel the same. As with personal relationships, you have to work through both the good and bad times to make a professional relationship work.

> "Managers who are skilled communicators may also be good at covering up real problems."
>
> Chris Argyris, Harvard Graduate School of Education

You must be comfortable with potential professional contacts on a personal level as well. If people have personal problems, the problems will overflow into their work life no matter how hard they try to hide them. Alcoholism, drug use, family troubles, and personality disorders will all emerge in the workplace and affect everyone's work performance and relationships. Any time you deal with people, remember you have to look for warning signs just like you do when you date.

One rep says that when she first saw her interviewing manager, she thought he looked "sleazy." But during the interview he presented the product so well and seemed so knowledgeable that she ignored her gut instinct. Guess what? After she took the job, she found out that he was in fact a sleazy person. He told her one thing and then did another. She spent an entire year putting up with his lack of ethics, before finally leaving. If she had just trusted her instincts, she would have taken another position and could have avoided the whole unfortunate situation. She resolved that if in the future she felt uneasy or had a bad feeling about a manager, she would trust her instincts.

"One who gains strength by overcoming obstacles possesses the only strength which can overcome adversity."

Albert Schweitzer

Remember this is not meant to discourage you, but to give you a warning about what could happen if you are not aware of the pitfalls of the sales field. Unfortunately until you get out there and take a stab, you will never know if you have what it takes to avoid them. Not everyone goes through these types of problems, and most opportunities in the marketplace are truly great.

Finding a sales job means you must take one day at a time and remember to stay focused on your goals. If you start to feel overwhelmed, take a break for a few days, then start back. Make a list of things to do each day, week, and month, and if you don't do everything, add it to the top of your next list. You must stay focused, be persistent, and don't let rejections undermine your confidence. Success can and will happen.

"The profession that makes up the largest percentage of people earning over $100,000 a year is sales."

Bradley G. Richardson,
Job Smarts
50 Top Careers

Finally, to make sure things go as smoothly as possible, remember to research thoroughly, trust your instincts, ask lots of questions, interview with lots of companies to find the right position, get everything in writing, and then *have fun* in your new career.